QUANTUM
SPIRITUALITY

Amit Goswami, Ph.D.
and
Valentina R. Onisor, M.D.

BlueRose
Publishers

Also by Amit Goswami

The Self-Aware Universe
Science and Spirituality
The Visionary Window
Physics of the Soul
The Quantum Doctor
God Is Not Dead
Creative Evolution
How Quantum Activism Can Save Civilization
Quantum Creativity
Quantum Economics
The Everything Answer Book
Quantum Politics
(With Sunita Pattani) The Quantum Science of Happiness

Also by Amit Goswami and Valentina Onisor
Upcoming books

How You Can be Your Own Quantum Doctor
The Quantum Science of Love

QUANTUM SPIRITUALITY

The Pursuit of Wholeness

Amit Goswami, PhD
Valentina R. Onisor, MD

First Published in November 2019

ISBN: 978-93-5347-933-6

Price: INR 295 | USD 14

BLUE ROSE PUBLISHERS
www.bluerosepublishers.com
info@bluerosepublishers.com
+91 8882 898 898

Figures:
Terry Way

Cover Design:
V. R. Onisor

Typographic Design:
Debabrata Dey Biswas

Distributed by: Blue Rose, Amazon, Flipkart, Shopclues

This book is dedicated to
the spiritual awakening of Humanity

Table of Contents

Foreword

The word "quantum" is largely absent from the life of the average person, and even physicists, who have used it for over a century, take off their white lab coats at night and go home leaving the quantum behind. Persuading us that the quantum is important for spirituality and healing is the object of the book you are holding, and I'd like to offer some opening ideas to pave the way.

The quantum needs to pass what has been called the "So what?" test. That is, it must expand from theory into something practical and useful. Most scientific discoveries pass the "So what?" test by leading to a new technology, and the quantum achieved that long ago—human creativity owes both the atom bomb and the transistor to quantum physics, just to mention two early applications. But this isn't the same as applying the quantum to ourselves personally, which is what quantum healing or quantum enlightenment, two of the main subjects in this book, are all about.

Strange to say, we are entangled in the quantum domain already, whether we notice it or not. Every physical object in the universe emerges from the quantum field, including our own bodies. This fact has been recognized for decades, yet it has had no real impact on the average person, who simply assumes, if he thinks about it at all, that "going quantum" just involves reaching a level of the physical world tinier than atoms and molecules. We don't define ourselves, outside textbooks at least, as being atomic and molecular, so the quantum doesn't impinge on our daily lives, either.

But here we've jumped to a false conclusion. In its search for the tiniest building block in creation, a project going back to the ancient Greeks, the human mind investigated Nature by reducing its to smaller and smaller things, on the assumption that big things are just an accumulation of small things, the way a beach is composed of grains of sand, a coral reef of tiny one-celled organisms, and the human body of trillions of cells.

This assumption breaks down at the quantum level, and it's a good thing that it does. Unlike atoms and molecules, quanta exist at the pivot point between nothing and something. They have double personalities, emerging from a vacuum first as invisible waves with no definite location but then coalescing into particles. The particle side of their nature gives us the physical world, but the wave side of their nature is much more mysterious. It is involved in a process physics calls "something from nothing," which is the most primal act of creation and the ultimate magic trick.

Being the first step in creation, something from nothing defies common sense—a stage magician pulls a rabbit out of a hat because the rabbit is hidden in the hat to begin with. But the nothing that produced the universe is impenetrable. It contains the potential for our universe and perhaps a myriad of other universes. It somehow organizes creation in such a way that 13.8 billion years after the Big Bang, there is human DNA, the most complex molecule in the known universe. Most mysteriously of all, nothing gave rise to mind or consciousness.

You can spend a lifetime trying to understand how the quantum domain does all of these things; if you think about it, producing something from nothing lies at the heart of any question anyone has ever asked. But if we focus on the personal, something from nothing is exactly how thoughts, emotions, perceptions, memories, insights, curiosity, and creative leaps occur. Every thought is preceded by a blank space and followed by another blank space. In this gap something emerges from nothing.

Therefore, if our bodies and minds are quantum creations, constantly being renewed, this opens up huge possibilities for what it means to be human. Amit Goswami and Valentina Onisor lay out the details of how every person's interaction with mind, body, world, and cosmos is a quantum interaction. Their exploration is fascinating and in my opinion harkens a new, expanded vision of medicine, psychotherapy, biology, genetics, and much more. We are on the verge of redefining what it means to be human, and Goswami and Onisor are on the forefront of this revolution.

But there's a catch. Until we understand what "nothing" actually consists of, "something" cannot be understood, either. Without an origins story, our relationship to Nature and our place in the universe remain a riddle. Drawing on insights that go back thousands of years, one discovers that "nothing" poses an either/or choice, in fact, the most basic of either/or choices. Either the "nothing" that gives rise to "something" is empty or it is full.

The option of seeing "nothing" as empty is tempting to all who believe that creation began with the Big Bang, a swirling super-heated chaos that led over time to the cosmos, in which the (still mysterious) action of random events controlled by physical laws led to life on Earth. This view of "nothing" has been part and parcel of mainstream physics and cosmology for a long time, even after the quantum and its ghostly existence pulled the rug out from under simple materialism. There is no smallest thing from which big things are made, a fact that gets conveniently overlooked by countless working scientists. Eventually, stymied by the impossibility of getting any data from "nothing," physics resorted to advanced mathematics as our only hope for explaining what happens in the womb of creation, thereby removing "something from nothing" totally out of the realm of everyday life.

The other choice in this either/or setup is fullness, the proposition that far from being an empty void, "nothing" is the field of infinite possibilities. It is the origin of every quality known to the human mind, including the qualities we value most in our lives: love, intelligence, creativity, evolution, discovery, etc. If the fullness choice is right, then every moment in our lives is connected to our origin. The startling conclusion to be drawn is that if the field of infinite possibilities is actually present here and now, the human mind must be partaking of infinity, not just in some exotic way scribbled in long equations on a black-board but as our normal way of living.

This definition of "nothing" as fullness goes back to ancient India and from there gave rise to religion-based spirituality—it was a small step from infinite fullness to an infinite God or gods. But assigning creation to a supernatural being misses the original insight, which is that fullness in consciousness—called Wholeness in this book—gives each of us a connection to infinite possibilities. At bottom, the human potential movement is based on this insight, which Goswami and Onisor unfold with intelligence, compassion, and optimism.

Their fund of knowledge is hugely impressive, and Quantum Spirituality is a milestone book. There is no saner, more convincing book on the emerging phase of human evolution—an evolution in consciousness open to everyone.

Deepak Chopra, MD

Preface

After researching quantum physics and its extension quantum science for several decades I, Amit, can declare: quantum science can fill in all the gaps in the incomplete science practiced today by most scientists under the aegis of the metaphysics of scientific materialism - "matter is everything". Under this straitjacket, these scientists miss out on the science of consciousness, life, feelings, meaning, intuition, creativity, paranormal phenomena, evolution, reincarnation, and spirituality. Quantum science, based on the primacy of consciousness, explains all these phenomena.

Most importantly, quantum science is rooted in creative discoveries made in India at least five thousand years ago. The latter has given rise to esoteric wisdom traditions in India and elsewhere as well as exoteric religions where indeed, many dogmas cloud the wisdom. Quantum science fills in the gaps of the wisdom traditions as well by explaining the interface of spirit and matter, an interface that is traditionally called "the subtle world".

The wisdom traditions speak of spirituality as basically an exploration of the nature of the self, Who am I? Quantum science reveals that although this is the highest aspiration for a human being and leads to liberation from suffering through the foibles of the human condition forever, most people, in the olden days and now, are not ready for this lofty exploration. Quantum science points to a step-by-step approach to spirituality for worldly people to serve the world staying within the world until they are ready for the cessation of all flames of desire and liberation from the world.

I discovered that the spiritual journey staying in the world, by and large, can be approached as a journey of progressive expansion of consciousness to include others, an expansion that we experience as happiness (to be distinguished from pleasure which often consists of a contraction of consciousness such as sadism or alcohol consumption). Accordingly, I wrote a book with psychologist Sunita Pattani and named it *The Quantum Science of Happiness*. The book will be released in early 2020.

In 2017, while I was teaching an advanced quantum activism workshop in Sao Paulo, Brazil for a select few, an 'aha' insight came to me. The journey in happiness very soon becomes a journey of exploration of what we call spiritual values or archetypes: love, beauty, truth, abundance, power, goodness, justice, wholeness, and self. Exploration of self liberates you from the world, as I said above. On that day I realised that if instead, we explore the archetype of Wholeness, then we can forever stay in the world because the journey in wholeness, unlike the journey of self-exploration, has no end. I also realised that this then, is the meaning of the Bodhisattva vow in Buddhism - staying in the doorway of liberation until every sentient being is ready for it. I realised additionally that this is the spiritual path that the great teacher Sri Krishna taught in the Bhagavad Gita carved and the great mystic/ philosopher Sri Aurobindo developed further. I realised that the time has come to scientize this path to spirituality because of its appropriateness for the twenty-first century spiritual aspirant.

There has been an age-old spiritual path for worldly people called Tantra that uses vital life energies to explore the archetypes rather than the mind and meaning. My co-author, Dr. Valentina R. Onisor, MD, is an exponent of both the art of medicine and integral esoteric spirituality, integrating vital energy knowledge and methods in her life and work. She was invited to attend the Quantum Activism workshop in Bangalore, India in 2016, and ever since, we have been researching and teaching mainly that what is popularly called the problem of integrating the head and the heart. Naturally, she joined me in this enterprise of developing a spiritual path for exploring Wholeness. It helped much that as a physician by training, she has been exploring Wholeness in her medical practice for several years, integrating conventional and alternative medicine. This is how it works when the shoe fits.

Who is this book for? It is for everyone. Let's count the ways:

- For the young reader, this book will bring meaning and purpose to your life.
- For the professional in general this book will help you integrate how to think, how to live, and how you earn your livelihood; in other words, this book will help bring congruence in your life.
- For the medical professional in particular, this book will help you practice health and healing as restoring wholeness.
- For the leaders in business, politics, or social activism in particular, this book will teach you how to integrate your outer creativity with inner transformation and how to explore abundance and power with social good in mind.
- For the middle aged people confused about how to make the midlife transition this book will provide you a worldly path to spirituality.
- For all spiritual aspirants, this book will provide you with an alternative way of enlightened living.

Chapter 1

Introduction: The Need for a Scientific and World-Affirming Spirituality

The subtitle of the book should intrigue you. Usually, spiritual traditions talk about enlightenment as synonymous with self-realisation - the moment you realise that you are not your ego but a cosmic consciousness. What they don't tell you (hush! Close the doors), is that there is utmost joy in that state, but no self to enjoy it! In this book I show you the steps to find a state of enlightenment to live where the joy is somewhat compromised but you are still there, you get to enjoy it. Are you interested?

If you don't know me, I (Amit) am a quantum physicist, consciousness researcher, and a quantum activist. I teach quantum activism workshops all over the world. Quantum physics has unambiguously integrated science and spirituality; I teach people how to transform their lives and the world accordingly.

Dr. Valentina is a practicing physician specialised in Family Medicine. With over 16 years of experience, she has successfully incorporated various branches of ancient and modern integrative healing systems (quantum healing, acupuncture, ayurveda, aromatherapy, apitherapy, tachyons, naturopathy, new German medicine), consciousness development methods such as esoteric yoga and meditation, into her life.

We wrote this book throughout using the first person, I, but be assured, it is the voice of both of us that you hear.

In quantum physics, objects are possibilities residing in a domain of potentiality outside of space and time. In this domain, no signals are required for communication when two objects are in a state of correlation or entanglement; communication is instantaneous. Such instant communication is forbidden in space and time, where communication must take place through exchange of signals and that has a speed limit. Communication takes a little time for signals to go through the distance that separates the objects. In contrast, the domain of non-locality-signalless communication - is a domain of potential unity. Closer examination reveals that this domain of potential unity is consciousness and its potentialities. And the domain of space and time is what consciousness experiences by becoming immanent and separating itself into a self (subject) and the other (objects) in the process of converting potentiality into manifestation.

This is how quantum physics integrates science and spirituality. Spiritual traditions have been saying for the past five thousand years that there is a domain of reality transcending space and time, a domain where all is one. What we experience as immanent is secondary to that.

If consciousness is the nonlocal ground of being, all our experiences - not only physical sensing, but also nonphysical thinking, feeling, and intuition - must come from it. This extension leads us to what we call quantum science. Thinking brings meaning back in science, intuitions bring back purpose such as love, and feelings bring back passion in our exploration of meaning and purpose. In this way, the extension of the ideas of quantum physics to quantum science further opens the scope of integration of science and spirituality. In fact, it gives us a new conceptual lens to sort out all our experiences - sensing, feeling, thinking, intuition, and spiritual. In this way, quantum science gives us the quantum worldview, a new lens for human beings to view the world, about which I have explicated a lot in earlier books.

People come to our workshops because there is a real hunger in people today for meaning and purpose in their lives. This is partly a consequence of the prevalent worldview of scientific materialism, the idea that everything is matter and the play of material interactions. In that view, the concept of information - other people's meaning - dominates ordinary people's psyche. And according to these elitists who dictate people's experience of meaning (or the lack of it), the world is seen as mechanical and cause-driven with no purpose.

This would not be so bad because there is the other worldview, religion - and religions ought to be providing its followers (fifty percent of the world's people) with some sense of meaning and purpose. Wherefrom religion? The spiritual wisdom traditions did not sit well with ordinary people who could not comprehend its subtleties; religions are popularised versions of the spiritual traditions. Unfortunately, especially in the West, religion gives a confusing message. It does not reject purpose entirely; but it propounds that the ultimate purpose of human life is to strive for living in perfection - in the company of an entity separate from us called "God." God is transcendent - outside of space and time; that's the part Western religions emphasise. We cannot go to God's abode – heaven - unless we earn virtues, so there is purpose. The fruit of our action arrives only when we die. In this way, religions tend to be world-negating, even life-negating; not appropriate for people of a time when after hundreds of years of science and technology we have finally learned to cope with the environment to a large extent.

By reaffirming that God is available and immanent also in the world and in us and also giving us the means of exploring our God-ness, the quantum worldview points to a middle path between world-affirming but God-negating materialist science and God-affirming but world-negating religion. There is happiness in the world and life after all! Not only from material pleasures but also from the immanent spirit.

And therefore in this book we declare: *the meaning and purpose of human life for most people is served best if they adopt this middle path consisting of integrating science and spirituality in their lives, explore meaning and purpose, achieve integration, inclusivity, and Wholeness, and live and serve in the world in a flow balanced and harmonised between the world and immanent God, the spirit.*

There is neither religion nor science that is superior to the Truth. Modern materialist science and feudalistic religions are in horns because they both are claiming to approach the Truth and that their way is the right one. This apparent contradiction is possible to solve only if we are going to realise the fact that both the scientist and the mystic have to orient their aspiration towards the same God (for materialist science, there is no God, but there are the material laws of science which govern matter) and to seek to know God or Absolute Truth together, in a spirit of fraternity. When the scientist and the mystic work together, they have all the tools that are needed for the delicate task that they both are assuming. The scientist has the proper "equipment" and the mystic has the desire to go explore the "map of the place". Until they understand that only together they have a chance, their work is the work of the two impaired people trying to find the way out of a labyrinth, one having good legs but being blind and the other one having good eyes but no legs. No matter which method we use or what the philosophical explanation is of what are we doing, the reality of our experience is the same. In summary, scientists should take mystical experiences as data to be seriously considered for validation. Then the collaboration between the scientist and the mystic will lead to the rebirth of the ancient spiritual science, from the times when the one with a scientific spirit was devoted to the Supreme Goal and the one with a mystic heart was thoroughly studying how to reach there.

Are we proposing a new religion here? Categorically, no. We are proposing a new way of living. It is not a coincidence that the idea of this new form of spiritual living integrated with science came to me while Valentina and I were teaching a quantum activism workshop in Brazil on Life Management- "How to manage your life using the quantum principles and worldview." The participants of the workshop were co-discoverers.

The Stuff to Integrate and Arrive at Wholeness

The idea of immanent spirit is not entirely new. What is new is the integration: we do not leave the transcendent out either.

The exploration of Wholeness in our life can begin at many levels. There are many dichotomies in the way we live and relate that prevent Wholeness. To arrive at Wholeness, to make a start, is to integrate the major dichotomies of which there are three. Read what Jesus said two thousand years ago:

> *When you make the two one,*
> *and when you make the inner as the outer*
> *and the outer as the inner,*
> *and the above as the below,*
> *and when you make*
> *the male and the female into a single one*
> *so that the male will not be male*
> *and the female not be female,*
> *then shall you enter the Kingdom.*
> *(Thomas: p. 17)*

The "kingdom" is the kingdom of heaven of course. Above and below stand for transcendent and immanent. Transcendent is what in quantum science "we call domain of potential non-locality" (signal-less communication) and immanent is local space and time (where communication requires signals). *Inner* refers to our internal experiences of feeling, thinking and intuiting, *Outer* refers to our external experiences of sensing. Jesus' emphasis is clear though: entering heaven is the goal of the integration of the dichotomies. And this is what I am proposing we dis-emphasize. For us, the integration of these fundamental dichotomies is important because it leads to Wholeness and harmony in our dealings with earthly matters.

In quantum activism and in the institutes of transformative education that our friends and I have founded, we emphasise achieving congruence of thinking, living, and making livelihood, to arrive at Wholeness.

Thinking refers to the worldview you are using to think whether you are aware or not you, we all, wear a lens to sort out the experiences that happen to us, and that is our worldview.

Living refers to how we actually experience and live our lives. Scientific materialists try to sell the idea that we are robots, determined machines; we live programs built into us by evolution, the genes, and some role is allowed to our socio-cultural environmental upbringing as well. Robots can sense stimuli, operate programs in response, and can process information. Materialists emphasise sensing, the negative emotional brain circuits, the brain circuits of pleasure, and information processing. Materialists admit, robots cannot possibly have experiences for which one needs a subject or self - the experiencer. Neuroscientists categorise us as philosophical robots, p-robots for short, robots with experience. Go figure.

Of course, pragmatic people, even materialists, don't actually live this way as p-robots, especially, the elites. They process meaning, even feeling like that of romance and infatuation with power; even value intuitions and archetypes like Abundance, Power, and Love; only that they say it is pretend, they may even believe that. That philosophy - our nonphysical experiences are pretend experiences - by the way, is called *existentialism*.

In the quantum worldview, all our experiences are scientific, not just sensing and information processing. We sense, feel, think, intuit, the whole gamut. We are not robots living on memory built into us; we can be creative and explore the totally new. Our dreams have meaning. We even process in our unconscious. This full scope of living can only be realised if you think with a wider lens. Now do you see? This is why you need the quantum worldview to think with.

What else do we need to integrate to achieve Wholeness? A major facet is thinking and feeling. Culturally, men emphasise thinking, women emphasise feeling. This one is interesting because for a long time I thought that the neocortex is the only place where we experience a self separate from the object we are experiencing. And neocortex is built to process mental meaning. I thought we cannot experience feelings without thoughts. Feeling plus thought is called *emotions*. Our common experiences of feeling are indeed via emotions.

You know what? I know better now. In 1983, I was attending a workshop by the physician/spiritual teacher Richard Moss. Richard himself with his colleagues gave each one of us a "chakra healing." Chakras are supposed to be points along our spine where we experience feelings. Well, afterwards, there was a session, and people, there were twenty-six of us, were telling their experiences in glorious terms. I, who had hardly any experience, felt totally left out. Like "what am I doing here?" Finally, I could not hold it any longer and raised my arm.

"Yes, Amit?"

"Richard, looks like you gave all these experiences to all these people, why not me?"

Richard said, "Amit, I can only open the door for you.

It is you who has to pass through it."

"Sounds well and dandy. So you are saying all these people passed through the door and I chose not to?"

"That's for you to decide. All these people left their selves at the door. That's the trick. Then you enter."

"But I am a scientist. I want to be there when it happens," I blurted out. Everybody was laughing 'LOL' in today's language. And I realised my mistake. In the next few days I received ample doses of Richard's prescription medicine - juicy physicality consisting of intimate hugs, especially from women. After that and a few more sessions of chakra healing, I got it. I could experience - feel - energy in my chakras in the body.

Of course, it is undoubtedly true that experiences come with two poles- subject and object, self and the other. If you don't see this, meditate. In mindfulness meditation, you can easily see yourself (your "I") looking at thoughts in your internal sky. Of course your looking has converted the "I" you are looking at into a "me," but the "me" has an implicit flavor of "I." Got it? The confusion is created because ordinarily our "I" experience gets mixed up with the "me." What we call *our ego* is really I/me. If you persevere in mindfulness meditation and always try to look for the I that is looking at the I/me looking at the I/me ad infinitum, occasionally you feel relaxed. What relaxed you? You fell into a state of the self (call it *quantum self*) much closer to the unity experience, hence of much expanded consciousness. When you have this kind of experience, it is natural to conclude that there is a quantum self which is pure 'I' with no 'me'.

I have such experiences of relaxation regularly. Many people do even better regularly. They regularly experience the pure I, *no me*. It is now even codified. The researchers Daniel Goleman and Richard Davidson have written a book on long term meditators, *Altered Traits*, whose brain imaging clearly shows the distinction that they are experiencing pure "*I*" rather than the I/me of the ego much of the time. This pure "*I*" is called *inner self* in spiritual traditions (*antaratman* in Sanskrit), transpersonal self in transpersonal psychology; in the quantum worldview, we call it the *quantum self*.

The book that put me on the map of consciousness research, The *Self-Aware Universe*, has all the details of how the understanding of quantum physics leads us to the explanation of how the brain - the neocortex - gets to have a self and how we get to have an experience. I will summarise the details of the theory in this book as well, but later. Suffice it to say, at first I could not see any such way of understanding a self in any of the chakras to qualify them as places where you have a self, have experience of pure feeling.

Materialistic people love only matter, because in their view, there is only matter and nothing outside of it. When asked how did matter appear, or why there is this matter, they will never give a complete answer. In this view, life has no meaning. When a human dies, he simply is gone, because "there is nothing like life after death". Until they experience it themselves, there are a few scientists that make headlines having changed their minds after having a near-death experience. They are too few.

Nevertheless, the immense majority of people are in search for happiness as their ultimate target in life. Most often, the happiness they find is superficial and ephemeral, hence people carry on again and again the hunt for lasting happiness in their illusory ways. All religions, philosophical systems, even politics in its own way, and science as well, are in the pursuit of the most beautiful illusion.

Those brain scientists - you got to give them credit. Recently, believe it, they have discovered two little brains in the body, huge bundles of nerves, one at the navel, the other at the region of the heart, exactly where two of the major chakras are supposed to be located.

"*Aha,*" thought I in a creative surprise. There are selves in the body after all, selves of pure feeling. The mechanism that gives the neocortex a self is available also at the navel and at the heart chakra. The selves there are weak to be sure; the brain self overwhelms them no doubt in the ordinary course of life. When intuitions come to them, many men talk about their "gut" feeling and many women talk about "intuitive knowing" with their heart. So there! these selves are not totally unfamiliar to us.

So there is another thing to integrate: the selves. Are there more? I brought up intuitions above. What do we intuit? The objects of intuition are so subtle that we can explore them only through our thoughts and feelings about them, but not in their suchness. We call them *archetypes* following Plato, elevated contexts of thinking and feeling.

An example will make the situation clear. Love is such an archetype. You think and talk about love every day, right? But do you know what love is for sure? It is like that Joni Mitchel song, isn't it: *I have looked at love from both sides now/from up and down and still somehow/it's love's illusions I recall/I really don't know love at all.*

There are nine major archetypes that concern us the most – including Love, of course. They are the highest thinking and feeling that humans can conceive. They are very much related with your *dharma*, your own chosen purpose of your life, therefore it is essential to discover and pursue them, inclusively for our state of well-being and for all what we call *integration*.

There is the archetype of Abundance that business people are meant to pursue. You probably think business people are meant to pursue money. Have you noticed that even if they go on making money, even to the extent of being billionaires, they are not satisfied. This is because these billionaires never feel that that they have made enough. In other words, they don't feel they have achieved abundance. The reason is they are not doing it right, the exploration of the archetype of Abundance.

You can never do it right with the archetype of Abundance if money is the only goal. It is like an episode of the comic strip *Pearls before Swine:* In the first frame, Burr (one of the human characters) says, "I am unhappy." He buys lottery tickets every day for ten years until he wins the lottery. Then he goes on a buying spree: cars, boats, a huge house. A later frame shows him saying, "I am still unhappy." He spends the rest of his life yelling at his pile of money, "Make me happy." The frame with the punch lines is so reflective of the materialist mind set. Goat says, "There is a lesson here somewhere." Rat says, "Probably needs a bigger house." And pig says, "Just buy more cheese!!!"

How do a few rich people become philanthropists? It is because they, in contrast to most of the rich people, have achieved greater fulfilment in their exploration of Abundance by seeking not only money but also meaning, passion, even archetypes like Love; they are doing the archetype of Abundance the full justice.

Then there is the archetype of Power. Politicians, business people, too, today, seek power. They, too, tend to be an insatiable bunch, don't they? They, too, are not doing it right. They seek power to empower themselves, not share it or empower others.

The same story goes for the five other major archetypes: Truth, Beauty, Justice, Goodness and Wholeness. (Self is the chosen archetype for monks, sadhus, and other renunciates - spiritual enlightenment seekers.) Under the worldview polarisation between religion and materialist science, the professions humans pursue have become so out of synch with their intended archetypes that nobody can find satisfaction with their professional pursuit anymore; or few do.

Which archetype should one explore? The mystic/ scientists of India discovered through their study of reincarnation the concept of *dharma* spelled with a small "d." We have a chosen archetype for this incarnation; that is *dharma*. Quantum science agrees with this: exploring dharma brings us satisfaction. If we ignore our *dharma*, if we don't start assuming consciously our role in this magical game of God and of creation, we become enslaved by our lack of purpose, we become drifters. *"Prisoner of senses, his existence lacks any meaning"*, says Bhagavad Gita (3, 10-16). A life without meaning is like death, life of a robot.

In quantum activism, we emphasise changing the professional world as we change ourselves so that we can earn a living via a profession which is in synch with quantum thinking and quantum living.

It helps to grade the archetypes in a ladder of very personal to very transpersonal (fig. 1). Abundance is at the bottom of the list because unless you have satisfied your survival needs, it remains personal: you want abundance for yourself with the exclusion of others. Power is next higher up; its pursuit is not as exclusive as that of abundance. And so forth for Beauty, Justice, and Love - progressively more inclusive of the "other." Goodness tips the scale; its pursuit is more transpersonal than personal.

We have not included the Truth archetype in this scale since truth is absolute, it cannot change from person to person nor can we give it labels like personal and transpersonal. It is sad that many people today think that truth is relative.

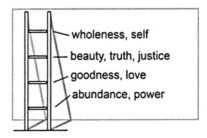

Fig. 1. The main archetypes (from personal to transpersonal)

The Archetype of Wholeness

The archetype of Wholeness is commonly the objective of exploration of the profession of health and healing mental and physical - at least to a minimal extent. A patient is sick when his or her body organs are not working in balance and harmony, although an allopathic physician today would perhaps not see it that way. In contrast in the quantum worldview, for true health, not just the physical but all the five "bodies" of a human being physical, vital (the source of the experience of feeling), mental, supramental or archetypal, and bliss (the unity) - need to be in balance and harmony.

Like other professions, the elite of the healing profession also makes it difficult for anyone in the profession to explore the archetype of wholeness and it would take quantum activism and a full-fledged paradigm shift to quantum integrative medicine to change things. Fortunately, this is under way.

The point though is that the archetype of Wholeness is much more than restoring physical health or even restoring mental health in the way we ordinarily understand it. In my recent book written with psychotherapist Sunita Pattani, *The Quantum Science of Happiness,* I have developed an optimal scale of happiness going from 0 to 6 (fig. 2); 0 for psychopathology, and 6 for the traditional self-realised, God-realised, enlightened people. In this scale, the realisation and embodiment of the archetype of Wholeness counts as happiness level 5, which puts it just a notch below the classic enlightenment of self-realisation. We call this *quantum enlightenment.*

However, there is another factor than happiness. Yes, all people seek happiness, no doubt. To live in the world, one not only needs happiness, but more so skilful action, intelligence. Intelligence to deal with any stimulus with optimal response which is what skill is about. The robots or artificial intelligence are good in informational and mechanical intelligence and that defines their scope. For human beings, this robotic intelligence makes you a human only marginally, even if you excel in it. Mental intelligence - the ability of meaning processing - is next and there are multiple sheds of mental intelligence depending on the various archetypes - implicit or explicit, each requiring its own brand of intelligence. Next come feelings. When we integrate mental thinking and vital feeling in the exploration of the world, especially relationships, we get emotional intelligence. When we dedicate our life to the archetypal explorations and embodiment within the overall archetype of Wholeness, we eventually head towards supramental intelligence.

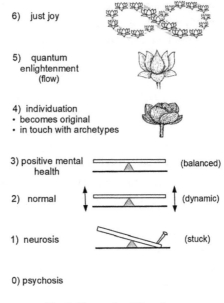

6) just joy

5) quantum
    enlightenment
         (flow)

4) individuation
• becomes original
• in touch with archetypes

3) positive mental   (balanced)
       health

2) normal   (dynamic)

1) neurosis   (stuck)

0) psychosis

Fig. 2. The scale of Happiness

In this way, quantum enlightenment becomes the ability to act with the highest intelligence available to humans - supramental intelligence a complete mastery over skilful action.

Time for a Paradigm Shift in Spiritual Exploration

In my workshops, I often ask the question to my participants, "How many of you want to be enlightened?" Usually, sixty to seventy percent of my participants would raise their hand in the affirmative. Then I ask, "Do you know what it means?" Of course not. When I explain that it means you will reach the highest state of happiness, no doubt, but that would be Being in unity consciousness in which there is no body to enjoy your enlightenment. That's when the enthusiasm drops down to zero.

You want enlightenment, perfect happiness, but you also want to enjoy it. That's your problem. You get confused because today there are so many spiritual masters, East and West, who claim to be enlightened, but do not live in unity consciousness most of their time. They sleep of course, but so do you. In sleep, we all go into undivided unity, but for most of us it is nothing special. We remain in the personal compartment of the unconscious, and God does not visit there. Is the state of sleep of these enlightened people special, that they get to be with God? It can be, but even so, it is only eight hours of living in Unity. If one lives the bulk of his or her time in separateness, would not the conditioning tend to come back?

Even more confusion exists in the training for the goal of enlightenment. You will be constantly reminded, Give up the ego. Drop the ego. How does one function in the world if one drops the ego conditioning? The great traditions are aware of all this, of course. There is a great Zen koan, How does the Zen-master go to the bathroom? If you give up the ego, there goes your toilet training!

Some masters rationalise that you give up ego identity, not the ego function. How do you retain ego's function, its conditioning and avoid the melodrama that conditioning creates? No wonder so many spiritual masters today get caught up in scandals.

It is time for a paradigm shift. If we make the archetype of Wholeness the goal of spiritual pursuit, not the highest happiness, but the highest intelligence as the goal of the human birth, what then?

What we will demonstrate to you in the rest of the pages is that with this goal all contradictions of the self-realisation path can be avoided. Yes, you can have your cake and eat it too. Just "compromise" on the quality of the cake a tad, from level 6 of perfect happiness to a happiness level 5. And you are getting something in return, highest intelligence we humans are capable of, greatest ability to act in the world with optimal skilfulness. How many times have you seen a so-called *enlightened* being lack in ordinary judgment? With quantum enlightenment, you will never have that problem.

In truth, spiritual traditions never intended for everybody to go for level 6 enlightenment of perfect happiness. There is a story about Buddha's encounter with a farmer. Buddha was trying to convince this farmer to become his disciple and go for enlightenment. The farmer asked, "Oh, noble Buddha. Your disciples have to renounce all worldly possessions and activities, do they not? And they have to beg for their living, right?"

Buddha replied, "Yes, of course. It is impossible otherwise to maintain congruence between thinking, living, and livelihood."

To this, the farmer said, "If everybody becames a renunciate, then to whom will your disciples go for begging for their food?"

Buddha realised his mistake and declared that for ordinary people, there is actually an alternative to perfect happiness. Complete satisfaction.

Look at Buddhism. Buddha's first noble truth says, "Life is suffering." No qualifications, just a flat declaration, life is suffering.

Do you experience life as suffering? Within the affluent societies of today, for young people of good health, the only suffering is boredom. Even that can be pushed under the rug by online shopping for a pair of shoes (for a woman) or a sports jacket (for a man). Ok, that is a joke, but not entirely. It is to avoid boredom that young people become information junkies only to discover later when big suffering hits as life begins to drift away in meaninglessness and purposelessness.

In the olden days, life was indeed suffering, especially for the ordinary people. No central heating, no electricity, no automobiles, no Internet. In that way, it was easy to be motivated to become a renunciate in search of perfect happiness. Today, most people are motivated only because they misunderstand all this. They do not realise what enlightenment entails, what giving up the ego means. I have talked to several enlightened people of the new age. One did not know what Nirvikalpa Samadhi meant or what God realisation - living in God entailed.

He had his experience but never thought of transformation that should follow. Another was worse. When a disciple asked, "What about emotions?" This man squarely replied, "Emotions do not exist." Enlightenment for him was all mind stuff !

Agreed, a few people may become bored after serving the world a long time, been there, done that. We reincarnate, you know. The quantum worldview supports the Hindu theory of reincarnation with scientific proof and empirical data amply proves the theory. The station of consciousness that we call *quantum enlightenment* and the ancients called *bodhisattva* state can be very long indeed extending over many incarnations. If you are truly bored in that way of living, and boredom is a suffering, who can complain if you declare, Life is suffering and take on the rest of the journey of self-realisation and God-realisation to make a grand escape? In reincarnation theory, once you are God realised, you do escape the birth-death-rebirth cycle, you are liberated. This I think is the goal of traditional enlightenment, to be liberated, to escape from manifest life when you are entirely bored with all worldly stuff.

Until then, let all spirituality minded people, and that means all people who see through the emptiness of life without meaning and purpose, explore the archetype of Wholeness, make their life congruent, integrate all dichotomies, and arrive at supramental intelligence via their exploration. The world will be a better place to live if that happens.

Buddha said, "ordinary people can opt for perfect satisfaction instead of perfect happiness". Dear reader, the exploration of the archetype of Wholeness is the way to perfect satisfaction. And yes, it can take you even further. When the fruit is ripe.

Chapter 2

Wholeness and I (Amit)

In my childhood, under the aegis of my father, I received a pretty good dosage of Hindu spirituality. My father was a Brahmin, a family guru; he had disciples who would occasionally visit him for "*darshan*." They would sit around him, and all would meditate. Afterwards, there would be what we would call a Q & A session.

I was also homeschooled by my parents. Sometimes, my father would speak of the Upanishads and its concept of Brahman - oneness of everything. I was fascinated, not that I understood. He had a good singing voice. So when he sang some of the Upanishadic sutras, I listened intently. One of my favorite sutras was this one. In Sanskrit:

Om purnam ada, purnam idam, purnat purnam udachyate.
Purnasya purnam adaya purnameba abashishyate.

Translation:

This is whole, that is whole. From whole you get whole. If you subtract whole from whole, you still get whole.

I was curious but did not comprehend much except the idea that underneath our separateness, all is one - Brahman which is Wholeness, *purnam*. The oneness appears to be separate as all of us individuals through the action of a mysterious force of illusion called *maya*. Since we are one Wholeness behind our illusory separateness, we should love one another. I got *that* message.

Even as a six year old, I'd see the contradiction. In my mother, for example. There was once a great famine in Bengal where I grew up; and there would be beggars all the time. My mother would often donate her own plate of food to a beggar, so kind was she. However, not always, especially not with my sister-in-law. Sometimes my mother would be so caustic with her that my sister in-law would cry, in private of course. But I had seen her crying many a time and I wondered, if we are one then why we can't love each other all the time.

There were riots, eventually a partition of Bengal took place as part of a deal that politicians had worked out while India was getting independence. I had to move with a part of my family to the Hindu side of divided Bengal. No more home schooling; I had to go to a public school for my education. And although history was my favourite subject I was also becoming fascinated with science. The idea of objectively verifying an idea before we make that a part of our belief system made sense to me. That's how I ended up in science.

Science meant materialist science even in those days, of course. Objects are made up of little atoms that make a little bigger molecules, and these molecules make up all the big bodies of the macro-world, including our physical bodies. What we see as a whole object, even that is not really a whole but made up of these little molecules and even littler atoms.

And that was just the beginning. Later I learnt that even atoms can be divided up further. The ultimate building blocks of material objects are elementary particles that you cannot break up any more.

All this made complete sense to me. There were theories, predictions, and data that verified the prediction. Compare that with the situation of the spiritual/religious worldview. Some people experienced something to be sure, then gave a theory of existence based on their experience that was contradictory to our ordinary experience. If there was underlying Wholeness and unity as they theorised, surely one prediction would be that we should be able to love each other. Obviously we are not capable of such love and that disproves the theory.

My friends and I argued about these things a lot as in our young hearts there was a lot of idealism and we wanted to see a loving society, a just society around us. In spite of the spiritual traditions and religions, the fact is people are so far unable to build a loving society.

What kept me hooked to the question for a long time was occasional confusion. When I was 8 years old, my father took me to the ashram of a local "enlightened" guru. The place was so full of something that I was instantly happy. When I asked my father, he simply said, "That's why we call the ashram sacred." Another intriguing concept, sacred. As opposed to what? "Mundane," said my father.

I pressed and he explained a little more. The goal of life is to explore the sacred, love, for example. How do we explore? We meditate.

I had seen my father meditate every morning. I tried to meditate following my father's instruction, but soon got bored. Then my mother intervened. "Amit is too young to meditate," she said to my father. And that was that.

Later, when I was in college and well on my way to give up the concept of Wholeness as the base of everything in favour of elementary particles being the base of everything, a sadhu appeared all of a sudden in our local boy's club and kept appearing. My younger brother and I would argue with him about the nature of reality and all our friends would join in. All of us against this fellow arguing in favour of spirituality and God. We would get exasperated but the fellow never lost his "cool."

One day, my brother harshly challenged him, "You keep telling us about oneness and all that. You got to give us a proof, a demonstration." The fellow looked at my brother for some time, then said, "I have heard you have a serious case of gastric ulcer, right?" My brother did indeed; he really suffered from it because my family ate hot tasty food and he could not eat it; he had to settle for bland food!

My brother was defiant. "So?" he enquired. "May I put my hand on your stomach?" said the fellow. "Okay," my brother said, a little contempt in his voice like sure, it's one of your hocus-pocus. The fellow calmly put his hand on my brother's belly for a few seconds, eyes closed. Then he withdrew his hand and declared, "You are healed."

My brother was not convinced of course. He immediately insisted and ate our regular cooking, really hot spicy food. Surprise! No reaction, no pain. He kept on eating hot food again; the ulcer did not bother him. No pain.

I was so impressed with this fellow for his capacity of administering spontaneous healing that I even took a mantra and instructions for meditation from him. Unfortunately, I still got bored and gave up. Meditation was not meant to be for me. Not then.

Fast forward to the nineteen sixties. I had received my Ph. D. and I was working as an instructor in physics at Western Reserve University (now Case-Western Reserve). My specialty was theoretical nuclear physics, applying quantum physics to uncover the mysteries of the internal dynamic of atomic nuclei. The Nobel laureate physicist Richard Feynman was my new hero and he was unequivocal about the nature of reality:

everything is made of atoms, and that includes us. Any theory that opposes that is wrong, like voodoo. For example, Freud's famous theory of the unconscious and conscious hinting at two levels of reality. Feynman was clear. Psychoanalysis is voodoo psychology, he said in his book, *The Feynman Lectures in physics.*

No worldview confusion for me anymore. Of course, there is only one level of reality - matter moving in space and time. Any underlying reality of oneness or Wholeness was voodoo, Feynman said so and it made sense. Matter based science will explain everything. If there is any substance to spirituality, matter-based theory would explain that too. I was convinced.

Fast forward again, to 1973. Confusion returned. My first encounter with the idea of Wholeness since young adulthood occurred in 1973 at a physical society meeting. I will tell you the whole story.

I was invited to an American Physical Society meeting to give a talk, which was considered quite prestigious. I gave my spiel and felt it went quite well but that feeling did not last long. As other speakers presented, I felt they were doing a much better job and naturally getting more attention, and I was jealous. The jealousy only increased during the course of the day. In the evening, I went to a party in honour of the speakers, and now I was getting jealous because others were getting more attention than my suave self from the women at the party. At 1 a.m., I noticed that I had consumed an entire packet of antacids, and I still had heartburn! I felt disgusted and went outside. The party was being held at a place called *Asilomar on Monterey Bay*. As I stood on the terrace, ocean air hit my face, and a thought came to me out of nowhere:

"Why do I live this way?" And at that very moment I knew. I knew I didn't have to live this schizophrenia between my life and how I made my livelihood. I could integrate. I could do happy physics. I could become whole again. I had discovered the goal for the rest of my life: it was to explore the archetype of wholeness. Archetypes - Wholeness, Love, and Beauty are examples - are the noblest contexts of our thoughts; even I at the time knew that.

Much later, when I was researching creativity, I found out that this kind of breakthrough is called a *crystallisation experience*. It is essentially that moment when you discover the archetype that you are destined to follow. The formation of a crystal from a solution is a little bit of a mystery. Experiences crystallise - a little mysteriously as well - into something that was potential in you. Reincarnation theory tells us that this potentiality, called *dharma*, spelled with a lower case d, is a choice that you make before proceeding with rebirth; and you bring suitable propensities from past lives to fulfil your dharma.

And here is the important thing: once again, *dharma* really is about spiritual values that religions call *virtues* and Plato called *archetypes* - intuitive objects such as Truth, Love, Wholeness, Abundance, Power, Justice, Goodness, and Beauty.

I have generally found this theory to be true. Before this experience, I was an ordinary, mediocre scientist. I excelled to some extent in my field of theoretical nuclear physics to be sure, but that was because nuclear physics no longer attracted the crème de la crème. And yet, after the experience, not immediately afterwards, but with some work, something changed. It was like there were abilities in waiting that now were reclaimed and I could do things that I never thought I would ever be able to do, among them solving the quantum measurement problem, integrating science and spirituality, integrating alternative and conventional medicine, developing a scientific theory of feeling, integrating all the different forces of psychology, developing a scientific theory of reincarnation, developing a scientific theory of life and its evolution, answering questions that molecular biology and neo-Darwinism could not address, even developing a new paradigm for capitalism. And in this book a new form of spiritual exploration suitable for our times. All these outer accomplishments pale in comparison to the transformation that took place in my character, like the capacity to love. Not instantly. Mind you, it took many years, but it happened.

I am getting ahead of myself. There were two other experiences that were crucial for my awakening. The first one of these happened in 1976, the second in 1985.

Let me give you the background for my 1976 experience. After the crystallisation experience of 1973, I began to make some changes to eliminate the obvious sources of unhappiness. That meant a divorce and a re-marriage on the personal living side and changing the area of physics research on the professional making-a-living side. Making changes on either side proved very challenging.

The first steps on the personal side was relatively speaking, easy. I divorced, I remarried a white American woman named Maggie, that was the easy part. The difficult part began even before my marriage was final. When I proposed, my woman said, "Yes, I will marry you. But I should tell you upfront that I love you but I am not in love with you." What's the difference? She added something which was even more intriguing: "There is something in you which is very pure and that attracts me very much. So, I say yes to marriage."

We got married but had a big fight even on our honeymoon. One thing led to another; she gave me an ultimatum - one year to put myself together. Now I understood: there must be a difference between loving and being in love. Maybe when one is in love, one is more forgiving!

Somehow, I managed to survive the year which was actually my sabbatical year at the University of Maryland at College Park. When we returned to Eugene, things settled down between us but she still would not say anything about being "in love." The challenge remained: How can I make this woman fall "in love" with me, whatever that meant?

The physics side also did not give any direct route to happy physics. One avenue I explored was science fiction. My physics department was trying to create new avant-garde courses for creating interest in physics for non-science students. I volunteered to give a course on the *Physics of Science Fiction.* The course passed the popularity test and it brought me in touch with many new physics ideas.

One of these ideas was black holes. Towards the end of their life, big stars collapse to become black holes from which even light cannot escape. A young physicist named Stephen Hawking, crippled by an unfortunate disease, was making fame with headline-grabbing discoveries about black holes. Maybe I could too.

Soon I realised that this would never integrate by life with my profession of physics since studying black holes had no practical living consequences. It makes good science fiction but makes no difference to how we live. It was more like what the medieval priests did according to legends, worry about how many angels could dance on the head of a pin.

One morning, I got a call from a woman in my class. Her name was Suzanne, she said, "Please meet me at the Student Union cafeteria after class today at 11:00 a.m. I want to show you something."

She sounded sincere. I went and was met by a woman in her thirties who promptly introduced herself and eagerly took my hand to guide me to the University Bookstore, some two blocks away. "There," she pointed at a book and said, "Buy that book." The title of the book was *The Tao of Physics* by Fritjoff Capra.

I was amused by all this and not a little touched by curiosity. I bought the book and Suzanne invited me to lunch the following day to discuss the book with her. "Would you mind?"

Why should I mind? I was married and loved my wife. I was not blind; she was very pretty. She said she was a divorcee; she must be lonely. Where was the harm in meeting a lonely pretty woman for lunch to discuss a book? No harm at all.

That evening, I read Capra's book for hours. It expressed the ideas of parallels between the current scientific thinking and the old spiritual thinking of the East - Eastern Mysticism. The more I read, the more enthusiastic I got. If there are parallels, why? My vision of integration, integrating my life and physics - my vehicle of thinking - came back to me.

Suzanne was another story but it sure seemed that she had led me to what I was looking for, the vehicle to integrate physics with life and that, I suspected, means integrating physics and spirituality.

My suspicion was soon confirmed. I had a dream that bothered me a lot, an unusual dream. In the dream I saw my father with a snake in his hand. As I looked at him in surprise, he threw the snake at me, and I caught it. He then disappeared. And I woke up.

So intrigued was I, that I talked to Maggie about the dream and she talked to her friend, Fleetwood. Fleetwood came to visit, and we talked for a while. "Dream images are symbols. They represent the meaning that you give to the symbol," said Fleetwood. "What does your father mean to you?" "A spiritual man," I said without hesitation. He was sort of a small-scale Brahmin guru with about a dozen or so disciples. Whenever I sat by him, I felt at peace, I told her.

Fleetwood became enthusiastic. "Your father represents the spiritual in you which is dormant right now. The snake on the other hand is a universal symbol, an archetype of the collective unconscious, a Jungian concept. It means transformation. The dream is an invitation for you to experience a spiritual transformation."

That jived with my vision to kindle my inner beauty so Maggie would "fall in love" with me. How does one attain spiritual transformation? I remembered what my father said when I was a child, "Meditate."

I started hobnobbing with various meditation groups. At the time Swami Muktananda was very famous and there was a group of Muktananda devotees in town who embraced me happily and I started meditating and chanting with them quite regularly. Nothing much happened except that after about a year of this I was getting bored.

Was there a way to meditate that would earn me quick results? A little research pointed me to a mantra meditation called *japa* which apparently people of my ancestral family practiced a lot. *Japa* is a simple repetition of a one-syllable mantra in your mind. After you do it for a while, the mantra is internalised. What that means is that the mantra goes on inside you somehow even when you are attending to other tasks. It was supposed to be going on while I taught or when I read a scientific paper. Once in a while, I'd check this out, and it was true. Whenever I checked, the mantra was right there. After implementing this practice for seven days, as I'd said, something happened. It was so special that I wrote down the experience:

"On a sunny November morning, I was sitting quietly in my chair in my office doing japa. This was the seventh day since I had started and I still had a lot of energy left. About an hour of japa, and I got an urge to take a walk outside. I continued my mantra deliberately as I walked out of my office, then out of the building, across the street, and onto the grassy meadow. And then the universe opened up to me.

... when meadow, grove and stream

The earth, and every common sight,

To me did seem

Appareled in celestial light,

The glory and freshness of a dream.

[W. Wordsworth]

I seemed to be one with the cosmos, the grass, the trees, the sky. Sensations were present, in fact, intensified beyond belief. These sensations were pale in significance compared to the feeling of love that followed, a love that engulfed everything in my consciousness until I lost comprehension of the process. This was Ananda, bliss.

There was a moment or two of which I don't have any description, no thoughts, not even feeling. Afterwards, it was just bliss. It was still bliss as I walked back to my office. It was bliss when I talked to our cantankerous secretary but she was beautiful in the bliss, and I loved her. It was bliss when I taught my large freshman class; the noise in the back rows, even the back-row kid who threw a paper airplane was bliss. It was bliss when I came home and Maggie hugged me and I knew I loved her. It was bliss when we made love later.

It was all bliss."

The feeling of all bliss did not remain for long. By the end of the second day, it started fading. When I woke the next morning, it was gone.

A comparison with the literature hinted that what I had experienced was called *Sananda Samadhi*, Samadhi with bliss, as an aftereffect. The Sanskrit word *Samadhi* stands for a convergence of the two poles of experience, subject and object. In our ordinary ego experience, the split of subject and object is huge and quite distinct. In my experience, in that split second, there was hardly a distinction.

Who was I then? The more stable ego-I, or that very special oneness-I that took seven days of meditation to precipitate? How could the brain produce both experiences? Also, the aftermath of the experience - *bliss* - came to me as a capacity to love anyone, an all-inclusive love. I was curious. Can one have this capacity to love not just temporarily but permanently?

Little did I know that I had hit the jackpot; I had experienced the archetype of Wholeness in its suchness – all-inclusive love, I had taken a quantum leap to a genuine creative insight in the same style as the author of the great Sanskrit line *Udaracharitanam tu basudhaiba kutumbakam* - to the person who has awakened to all- inclusive love, the whole world is family.

The third great and crucial experience of my exploration of Wholeness occurred in 1985 and this involved quantum physics. This is the subject of the next chapter.

To continue, below, Valentina will present certain concepts and a meditative exercise geared towards an experience of expansion of consciousness that at once gives us happiness or relaxation and inclusivity - the ability to include another in your consciousness.

Awareness and Relaxation

Awareness and Relaxation are very important and actually they are very interconnected. People usually associate awareness with contraction, tension. They associate relaxation with completely letting go, relaxing in the sense that you just go to sleep without being aware. The more we relax, the more aware we can be.

Awareness is not thinking, or intuition, instinct, moving, feeling. It implies to be awake in our life in each moment. The word itself comes from being a witness, aware of something, without judging. You notice old patterns falling away, as you experience more clearly your true essence, beyond your personas. The more we are aware, the more we relax and the less we are caught in emotions. An expanded awareness connects you with all resources, with the world around.

On the other hand, *relaxation* brings happiness of expanded consciousness. This kind of happiness (please learn to distinguish it from molecular happiness, call that one pleasure) begins with relaxation. If we are not relaxed, we are not happy. Also, the vital energy flows freely in association of a relaxed part of the body. If we keep for long periods a tension in the physical body, it will lead to a vital energy blockage and in time, even to illness. Relaxation is an active process - it does not happen by itself. We are not relaxed just by not doing something. We need to learn to relax actively. After relaxing at the physical-vital level, we relax at the mental and emotional levels as well.

In relaxation, you don't become numb, but instead you feel more and more alive. You may experience warmth, tinkling, vibrations. Not dull. Witness your inner aliveness, vitality, how you start glowing. It is not a switch off, but a switch on, without effort. You simply become present. It all happens in the NOW. Breath can also remove tensions and energise parts. If you feel tensed, you can relax fast by taking a few breaths.

Let's now scan our physical body - close your eyes, and simply "go" through your body with your awareness, looking for any tensed areas, jaw, belly, shoulders, and simply relax them consciously; allow the pelvic floor to sink down; relax your face. Take as much time as you need for this exercise. In the end, slowly open your eyes, breath deeply, give yourself a few moments to perceive the effects of this simple exercise. Then, get ready to take this state of awareness and relaxation in your activities throughout your daily life.

Chapter 3

The Quantum Physics of Wholeness

The author Fritjof Capra talked about Wholeness in *The Tao of Physics*; his approach to integrating science and spirituality was through the philosophy of holism as opposed to reductionism. Reductionism is a fundamental aspect of scientific materialism–the idea that things can be reduced to smaller and smaller objects until you reach the base level. In contrast, holism says this: a whole is always greater than the sum of its parts. The advantage of holistic thinking is this: you can claim all kinds of things to emerge from an assembly of objects. For example, how does the brain acquire a self ? You can say that the brain's self emerges as the whole that is greater than the parts - the neurons.

Can this be? Not really. Take the simple case of water. Reductionism says the water molecule can be reduced to two atoms of hydrogen and one atom of oxygen joined together by molecular bonding. Water is H_2O. Holists say no to this and they point to water's wetness as the emergent property of holistic water. This is cheating because the wetness comes from our experience of water; other interactions are involved.

Holism never appealed to me and yet I (Amit) thought Capra's point that there are parallels between spiritual thinking and some of modern scientific thinking is well- taken. The thought 'Why these parallels?' began to haunt me. Of all the different scientific theories in which Capra saw parallels with mysticism, quantum physics appeared to me to be the best candidate.

In the movie, *What the Bleep do we know*, I said a very poignant line: "Quantum physics is the physics of possibility". By then, it was 2003 when I was filmed, this depiction was acceptable to most physicists; but quantum physics was discovered in full in 1925-26 and in its early days the waves of quantum objects were called probability waves. The idea was to indicate that the waves help us calculate the probability of events, nothing more.

And yet, the quantum math does not work that way. To calculate using quantum physics you really have to constantly remind yourself that a single quantum object is a wave. For example, consider the famous double slit experiment. A bunch of electrons go through a double-slitted screen and fall on a fluorescent plate making a so-called *interference pattern* (fig. 3a). If we pass water waves through such a double slit arrangement, we get the same pattern. Hence the wisdom, the idea that electrons are waves is experimentally verified.

Is the waviness an ensemble property or a property of the single object? Here the math is clear. We really have to assume that every single object's wave splits into two waves that subsequently add as in algebra.

The addition gives different results at different places on the screen because the two waves travel different distances to a place and come with different conditions called *phase*.

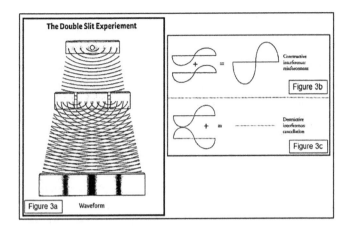

The Double Slit Experiement

Constructive interference: reinforcement

Figure 3b

Destructive interference: cancellation

Figure 3c

Figure 3a   Waveform

Fig. 3. (a) The double slit experiment (b) The interference of two waves producing constructive and (c) destructive interference

At some places, waves will come with the same phase (fig. 3b), there they will add and reinforce one another. The probability for arriving at these places will be large. At other places in between, the two waves will arrive in opposite phase and cancel each other out (fig. 3c), no wave in those places at all; probability is zero. And hence the pattern of alternative light and dark fringes.

Experiments bear this out. If we pass the objects through the slits, say from an electron source, so slowly that only one electron goes through at a time on the average, do we get a pattern expected of Newtonian objects, one pile behind one slit and another behind the other? No. Some of the electrons find their way to other places on the fluorescent plate; when enough of them collects, we get the interference pattern.

In this way, electrons, all quantum objects, are, each individually, waves period. They are waves of possibility. They become particles of actuality only when they arrive at a measurement apparatus, only when we measure. What we cannot predict from quantum math is where a single electron will arrive.

There goes another myth created by one of the pioneers of quantum physics, the physicist, Niels Bohr. Bohr rationalised. Since it is paradoxical - logically impossible - that quantum objects are particles as well as waves in space and time, Bohr proposed complementarity. Quantum objects are both waves and particles but you can see only one aspect in a given experiment. We must say no to that too. In the double slit experiment with a slow electron beam, the electrons can be seen to arrive at different places very particle-like, as dots; but they are not Newtonian particles, they fall all over the fluorescent plate in places that are not allowed for Newtonian particles. Only the totality of the dots look like a wave interference pattern. In this way, the same experiment is telling us that electrons are wave and particle.

Question: What determines where a single electron will arrive at the fluorescent plate? Here the scientific materialists play logical gymnastics trying to avoid an answer. The electron's behaviour is acausal, nobody can give a cause. Never mind that this amounts to giving up on one of science's most precious principle - causality. To produce an effect, there must be a cause.

Another tactic is to say, "Nobody understands quantum physics," this one from the great Feynman. No, you cannot understand quantum behaviour if you insist on the philosophy of scientific materialism according to which all causes are material interactions. No material interaction within the laws of quantum physics can ever convert a possibility wave into a particle of actuality, no matter how you try, how many instruments you use. This is called von Neumann theorem - 'the catastrophe of the endless regression', 'the relativity of instruments'.

To allow a non-material agency causally act on quantum waves from a domain of potentiality outside of space and time and converting them into particles in space and time is tantamount to giving up on scientific materialism. This, the early quantum physicists were unwilling to do. And even now, after three decades of my solution of the problem, most working physicists equivocate, there is too much social pressure. Fortunately, after retirement, many physicists change their minds, so support for a new quantum worldview among physicists is getting traction.

Plato's Cave

Truth, said Plato, is an archetype. We can see only a mental representation of truth, one facet, not all its facets at once. This is the problem. You may have read about the paradox of Plato's cave. As shown in fig. 4, the cave dweller is one who is strapped in a chair. He can only see what is projected on the wall in front of him, which is a shadow show. The shadows are representations of truer objects that Plato called *archetypes*. The cave dweller has to make an about turn to see the real archetype instead of the representations the shadow show created by the projector.

Fig. 4. The allegory of Plato's cave

Today, we call this old problem of the human mind by a different name: in-box thinking. Consider the following problem, called the nine points problem:

What is the smallest possible number of straight lines that will connect the nine points of a 3 X 3 rectangular array (fig. 5a) without taking the pencil off the paper?

It seems that you need five lines (fig. 5b), doesn't it? That's too many. Can you see right away how to get a smaller number of straight lines to do the job?

Perhaps not. Perhaps, like many people, you got stuck thinking that you have to connect the points while staying within the boundary defined by the outer points of the rectangular array. If so, you have defined yourself an unnecessary context for solving the problem, you are thinking in a box, and this is not the right box.

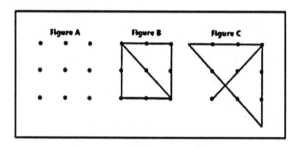

Fig. 5. (a) The nine points problem. Connect the points with as few lines as you can without raising your pencil. (b) The solution that first occurs to many people. They think within the box of their existing belief. (c) A better solution of the nine point problem. Think out of the box.

You have to move out of the box to find a new context in which a smaller number of straight lines will do the job (fig. 5c). This is a simple example of discovering a new context. This idea of extending the boundary beyond the existing contexts - thinking out of the box- is crucially important in creativity. Creatives beware! The implicit contexts for your problem may not be working, you may have to find new ones. And sometimes, creativity is that simple: just recognise that what is not forbidden may be allowed.

Richard Feynman called the box materialists wear a strait-jacket and yet he insisted that a physicist must wear this strait-jacket in order to do science. He could not see any way for doing science without this straitjacket. Feynman had taken many quantum leaps in his long physics carrier, but this quantum leap to leap out of the materialism box escaped him.

Probably Feynman had an antipathy to all philosophy including mysticism and spirituality that to the non-initiate does seem to be philosophical speculation. Contrary to Easterners, religions in the West do not put emphasis on the experiential aspect of mysticism. I was educated in both the East and the West. So although sold on scientific materialism, I had enough openness to hobnob with live mystics and that is what eventually led me to the breakthrough from the proverbial box.

Here is a story for the sake of completeness. As it happens, in May, 1985, I was talking about all this with the mystic Joel Morwood, formerly a film-maker. He was the associate producer of a notable film *The Jazz Singer* in the nineteen seventies. I was ranting: if consciousness is brain phenomenon, it is paradoxical; if consciousness is individual nonmaterial consciousness, it is paradoxical; if consciousness is (dualistic) God consciousness, it is paradoxical! What does a quantum physicist have to do to resolve the paradox?

The rest is history. We had a heated dialog. At some point, Joel asked, "is consciousness prior to the brain or brain prior to consciousness?

To this, I responded smugly (I am the physicist, he is just a film-maker!), "I know all about that. You are talking about nonlocality."

Indeed, as I have explained before, nonlocality defines the domain of quantum potentiality where waves of possibility reside; in this domain communication can be without signal, potentially instantaneous. Naturally this domain is outside space and time; what is prior to what cannot be asked.

Joel was acerbic, "You have scientific blinders on your head," he said. Then he shouted, "There is nothing but God."

Mind you, I have heard those words many times before; they are from Sufism, but all mystics talk like that. As Jesus said, "The kingdom of God is everywhere." And Hindus say,

"Sarvam khalyudam Brahman", all is consciousness. This time my internal response was unexpected, a total surprise to myself. I am thinking, suppose consciousness is the ground of being in the domain of potentiality and matter (including the brain) are possibilities of consciousness itself, what then. An about turn in my thinking? Yes, but who cares? I have solved the measurement problem.

If the nonlocal domain of reality that we call *potentiality* is consciousness - the one and only, all possibilities are its own - consciousness is choosing from itself, no signal, no energy exchange is needed, as nonlocality already suggests. All that is needed to start a new out-of-the-box thinking, a new paradigm, maybe even a new worldview, is to identify the nonlocal domain of potentiality with consciousness itself, the way mystics think, especially in the East.

It was like I was sitting in Plato's cave strapped in a chair, I could look only in front of me and see the shadow show of matter moving in space and time. I had figured from quantum physics that the shadows are cast by the waves of potentiality. I could not accommodate the thought that consciousness is casting the shadow by throwing light on the possibility waves, a metaphor for choosing, because of my prejudiced baggage that I carried. And now I could see it because the strap that bound me to look only forward was my own prejudice of scientific materialism. The moment I dropped the prejudice, the straps fell away, I made the about turn and saw the role of consciousness as the ground of all being.

What is the Non-Material Cause We are Looking For?

The physicist David Bohm became famous because to the popular Western mind, he gave us a model of God for modern times. He showed mathematically that if we make a simple approximation to the original quantum equations, the new equations that derive are deterministic but not materialistic;

there is now a new non-material force coming from an implicate order, a "quantum potential," that drives the movement of matter in the explicate order where we live. David Bohm's God is the agency of the quantum potential.

Later, the systems theorist Ervin Laszlo argued: *why not claim the same thing staying within quantum physics?* Why insist on mathematics and determinism? Laszlo proposed there is a nonmaterial quantum field that does the job of converting waves of possibility into particles of actuality. With all due respect, this line of thinking misses something very important.

Remember what I said in page 2? The domain of potentiality is a domain via which objects have the potentiality of communicating without signals, communication that we call *nonlocal*. If no signal is needed to communicate, there is no separateness, only unity. In this way, the domain of potentiality is also the domain of potential unity.

Quantum measurement splits up the unity into two: subject (the self of the brain) and object. Every quantum physicist until then had missed this; they only talked about objects. As the mathematician G. Spencer Brown observed:

We cannot escape the fact that the world we know is constructed in order (and thus in such a way as to be able) to see itself; but in order to do so, evidently, it must first cut itself up into at least one state that sees, and at least one other state that is seen.

The physicist John von Neumann came close though to my thinking this way in propounding the observer effect: without the observer, one cannot say a measurement has occurred. Indeed so. Von Neumann also correctly intuited how consciousness created experience, by choosing from the many-faceted potentiality and reducing it to one facet. He even intuited that the observer's self is what makes the observer nonmaterial, not bound wholly by material laws.

What is so special about the brain that consciousness identifies with it and become its self ? The brain has a tangled hierarchy, a tangled manner in which perception and memory create one another, that works like a trap. This tangled hierarchy makes the brain an irreducible whole. This is how holism becomes relevant. Of course, we experience our brain's self as a simple hierarchy - the head honcho of our conditioned habits and programs from which we choose our actions in response to stimuli. This creates confusion. I had to work all that out in my search for the meaning of quantum physics before going into print with my book The Self-*Aware Universe*. I will discuss all this in more detail in later chapters.

Can Quantum Physics Apply to Us?

The physicist John Wheeler said: *"the whole world with all its systems is quantic."* This suggests the fact that our concepts regarding the functioning of our own body will have to grant attention to the quantum physics. However, many biology researchers consider nowadays that the "subatomic events are too small to have a practical importance." Some scientists object in the same vein: "electrons and people are not the same thing".

Do materialist have a legitimate concern here? Quantum physics was discovered in connection with our scientific search for a theory of behaviour of the submicroscopic base level of matter. Matter is reductionistic, bulk matter can be reduced to elementary particles; and vice versa, bulk matter can be built from elementary particles. So no doubt that ultimately, quantum physics rules all matter, micro and macro. However, for practical purposes, we must recognise that for the bulk matter Newton's dynamics approximately holds. This, too, is part of the quantum dynamics applied to matter. What this means is that bulk matter is largely independent of consciousness, creativity and all that jazz.

What makes us think that somehow quantum physics applies to bulk living matter though its effect is negligible for bulk non-living matter? As I said in the very beginning, living matter is different, it has vitality. A living body is a dynamic duo of a physical component and a vital component. *It is the vital component that is quantum; the physical is quantum by association.*

Now let's go back to conceptualising the vital-physical duo, living bodies, as correlated quantum objects. They are one. When we experience a physical organ, we also experience the movement of its correlated vital organ (fig. 6). The experience of this movement is called *feeling*, right? Vitality, call it vital energy, is a feeling.

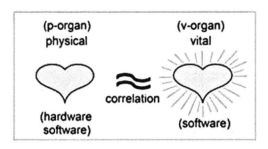

Fig. 6. Every physical organ (p-organ) comes correlated with a vital counterpart V-organ

We are saying vital movements are quantum; therefore, the movements of physical living bodies, the organs, are also quantum by virtue of correlation. How do we empirically know that vital movements are quantum movements?

There is a signature. Look at a physical object, say a chair, and imagine that a friend of yours is also looking at the chair. Although, the movement of the chair is ultimately quantum, and the center of mass of the chair does move by a measly 10^{-17} cm (don't worry, it has been measured by lasers), such small movements are quite invisible to your naked eye. So you and your friend see the chair at the same place and since this is shareable information you conclude that the chair must be outside of both of you. In this way you see the material world at the macro-level as outside of you.

In contrast, how do you experience feelings? As private and internal, right? This is because feelings are quantum. Between your feelings and your friend's feelings, the movement of the vital organ has changed so much in possibility that the two of you cannot likely actualise the same manifest feeling. In other words, you usually cannot share the same feeling with a friend. Feelings are private and so cognised as internal.

The mystic poet Kabir wrote:

Thinkers, listen, tell me what you know of that is not inside the soul [consciousness]?

Take a pitcher full of water and set it down on the water-

now it has water inside and water outside.

We mustn't give it name,

lest silly people start talking again about the body and the soul.

What is Kabir trying to say? That it is all consciousness, both psyche and *soma*. The difference of the water outside and the water inside arises from the glass boundary of the pitcher. The difference of psyche and soma arises from the different ways we experience them: we experience the physical world of *soma* external to us, but we experience also an internal world of awareness which we call the *psyche*.

Some of you, especially if you are a male, may be a little skeptical about the experience of feeling, but don't be. You, generally speaking, experience feelings mixed with thought; the mixture we call *emotion*. Emotions bring us passion, the juice of life. It's the feeling component in emotion that brings the juice.

Amazingly, the ancient wisdom traditions somehow intuited all this. In wisdom traditions, they always theorize that the Oneness which is called "the causal domain of reality" comes down to the material level called "the gross level" via an intermediary - called "the subtle level" (fig. 7). The subtle consists of not only the vital but also the mental with which we think (meaning) and supramental with which we intuit (archetypal contexts of elevated thinking and feeling such as Love, Beauty or Wholeness).

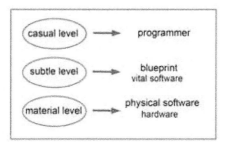

Fig. 7. Consciousness (the causal body) connects to gross (material body where representations are made) via the subtle (quantum potentialities mind, vital body, archetypes)

Thinking meaning is important for our wellbeing. When you are baffled and cry out 'What is the meaning of my life?' and no answer comes, you hit despair and become susceptible to diseases. And intuitions are invitations to explore the archetypes like love; they give our lives purpose. That, too, is essential for well-being.

It fits. Like feelings, we experience thoughts and intuitions internally as well, don't we? They, too, are quantum.

Wholeness

Now you see why the Self archetype gets all the attention from people who seek to know reality-consciousness without subject-object split. The self of immediate experience, the self that I call *quantum self*, acquires individuality through conditioning, personal history, personalities. In order to know the quantum self, as in the adage *know thy self*, we have to penetrate all that covering, and when we do, what do we find? The quantum self is empty of individuality, it is a pointer to that Oneness, the ground of being. This is the experience of self-realisation: there is no individual self, it is all Oneness.

And the task now is obvious: since the quantum self is a no-self, you have only two choices. Go back to the ego to live, or chuck it all, identify with the Oneness itself, and live there albeit it is unconscious. This is where things get difficult to comprehend. And philosophers over the ages have tried to explain things without logical inconsistency with varying degrees of success, but never complete success. In the quantum worldview, it is possible to "experience" the unity of the unconscious via delayed choice when conscious awareness is regained occasionally, to be fed and so forth. Read my upcoming book *See the World as a Five Layered Cake*, for details.

As I have said before, quantum physics enables us to understand things in a paradox free way, so what? You still end up living in the unconscious. Blissful that may be, but there is nobody to enjoy the bliss until you are awake and back to the ego.

The question, "Is there another way to experience the wholeness without having to be unconscious?" There is.

Empirically, researchers have found that four stages are required to precipitate a quantum leap of creativity and create a product: preparation, relaxation, Quantum leap of sudden insight, and manifestation. In this final stage of converting the insight into a manifest product, researchers find that there is a flow consisting of a seamless cooperation of inspiration and perspiration. The quantum worldview explains. The inspiration comes from the quantum self, the perspiration from the ego.

Got it? If we can harmonise creativity into our life on a daily basis, we can live in flow, in part quantum self. The ego is there but it serves the quantum self and experiences joy. We are having our cake and eating it also. How sweet life can be.

Our highest creativity lies in the exploration of the archetypes; among all the archetypes, Wholeness is the inclusive one, taking forever to fully manifest. I hope you now see why a paradigm shift is necessary for spiritual exploration, change emphasis to the archetype of Wholeness instead of the self-archetype.

Long ago, the Mahayana Buddhists floated the idea of *bodhisattva* with something like this in mind. Humanity was not ready and the idea did not catch. Now I think humanity is ready.

More recently, Sri Aurobindo also attempted to change the paradigm of spiritual exploration. In the Bhagavad Gita, four paths of self exploration are given: karma yoga with emphasis on service, raja yoga with emphasis on meditation, bhakti yoga with emphasis on love of the quantum self, and gyana yoga with emphasis on wisdom - via creative insight of the self. Aurobindo proposed Integral yoga - an integration of all these four yogas with another type of yoga involving feeling (traditionally called *tantra*). This is in the spirit of the exploration of Wholeness and inclusivity.

I hope you notice that my three experiences cover some of the same ground as Aurobindo's integral yoga. The first experience, 'Why do I live this way?' and the idea of integrating thinking, living, and livelihood refers to karma yoga, service to the world. The second experience used raja yoga, meditation and bhakti yoga, the mantra I used was a devotional mantra. The third experience when the wisdom Consciousness is the ground of all being and science can be done on this basis dawned on me was clearly gyana yoga.

I was lucky. All this happened without much understanding of what was happening. It has taken me forty years to understand and it is that understanding that we are sharing with you in this book.

Creativity

"Creativity is the discovery or invention of something new of meaning and value", said the creativity researcher Theresa Amabile.

Notice there are two words we conventionally use to denote creative innovation - discovery and invention. Why two? What is the difference? Invention refers to creativity in an already existing archetypal context. Discovery, on the other hand refers to creativity in a new archetypal context. The former I call *situational creativity*; the latter *fundamental*. The former can be carried out with a teacher's or guru's guidance;

the latter cannot, you are more or less on your own although a teacher can be your collaborator or your inspiration.

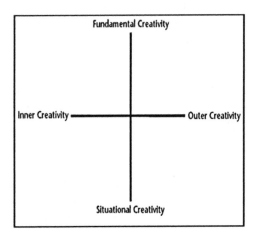

Fig. 8. Creativity has four poles

Even more important is to recognise that the process spiritual traditions use for spiritual exploration is the same as the creative process; it just has not been recognised as such creating much confusion. Creativity used for spiritual transformation we call *inner creativity*, creativity for outer accomplishment outer creativity.

In this way, creativity has four poles (fig. 8). All four poles are important; all have to be used in the exploration of Wholeness. Why do we suffer from uncontrollable negative emotions? Because socio-biologists are correct; these evils are built into us as brain circuits. Inner situational creativity is important for building positive emotional brain circuits to balance the negativity.

Today's young people suffer from an overdose of information processing and many of them are trying to come back from information to meaning processing to reinvent the meaning of their lives. Here again all they need is inner situational creativity.

As we noted earlier, the professions humankind engage with are all based on archetypes; our whole civilisation is a progressive exploration and embodiment of the archetypes. Under the influence of scientific materialism, the professions have become jobs to make money, and use the money to find entertainment; for what else is life but "eat, drink and be merry" in that philosophy? To make your profession into an exploration of archetype once again, you have to engage situational creativity, outer at first, but then increasingly inner, leading to embodiment, manifestation of the creative insight in your life. It behooves you to have a teacher or the traditional guru at this stage.

Finally, to creatively experience an archetype in suchness, you have to engage fundamental creativity; there is no substitute for that. And for this, there is no given path; so a teacher or a guru is not of much help.

This goes for the archetype of Self as well, for traditional spiritual enlightenment.

The myth of the *guru*, of course, continues. In a Frank and Ernest cartoon, Frank and Ernest are seen climbing a hill on the top of which sits a guru. Says Frank, "We need to see him because there is no satellite-based system to guide us on a trip down the path of enlightenment." Sorry Frank. He can't help you either! On this one, the mystic Jiddu Krishnamurti is right, "Truth is a pathless land."

Chapter 4

The Human Condition and How to Get Out of It

There is a story in the Upanishads of India, very telling about our need to transform. The simple hierarchical me-centered aspect of the human ego-persona is called *manava* in this story. This is the aspect that makes us miserly.

The *danava* aspect in us is attached to negative emotions, especially the one of domination; this is the aspect that makes us cruel, violent, and dominating in their search for pleasure.

To Hindus, the part of us that is addicted to pleasure, is *deva. Deva* is the positive counterpart of danava.

One day, all three see a strange being sitting on a hilltop, a being of considerable wellbeing and power emanating from it. Naturally, "what's in it for me" speaks up in each of the aspects of the human being.

First, the turn of the manava. "What is your advice for me so I can have as much wellbeing as you?" The being says, "Da." It is an intuition you see, subject to interpretation by the mind. The manava understands in his own way. *Da* stands for the Sanskrit *datta*, meaning *give*. The human-person is constricted by the me-centeredness. He amasses wealth, but cannot share it. Giving expands consciousness. Giving opens the heart and balances the me-centered exploration of the archetype of abundance into some other-centeredness as well which is when our sense of abundance is fulfilled and wellness comes. This is transformation.

Next, the danava approaches and asks a similar question, "What do you advice so I can have as much power as you?" The being answers, "Da." The danava, too, understands the intuition in his own way. "Da" for him stands for the Sanskrit word *dayadhhama* meaning *have mercy*. Cultivate positive emotions like compassion to balance all that negative. That will require creativity, exploration of the archetype of Love and Goodness, and balance the exploration of Power to help others as well. This is transformation, too and thus the practice will drive you towards it.

The last to approach the being is the deva. Same question, same answer, "Da." The deva understands. For him, "Da", stands for the Sanskrit word *damyata* meaning *restrain*. Restrain yourself from too much pleasure. Then room will be made for creative exploration of the archetypes; in this way you will engage subtler forms of happiness that requires transformation.

Good recipes to be sure. Are they scientific? My research and exploration of quantum physics and consciousness for four decades tell me yes. First, let's reframe the story for our times.

The pleasure-centered aspect, the negative emotional aspect, the me-centered do-nothing hoarding, security minded aspect still dominates the human being in this twenty-first century with one addition. The lowest common denominator has now shifted to a machine aspect that has replaced meaning processing entirely by information processing. Let's call this by the Sanskrit word *yantrava*, machine-ness. What drives yantrava to information processing is aversion of boredom.

Now there is that powerful Being again on the mountain top. This time, the yantrava approaches first. "I seem to have lost my humanness. I miss meaning and purpose. What can I do?" The Being is more kind this time and spells it out: Look inward; accept the boredom you will experience initially. Boredom passes; and then you will discover the splendour of your internal experiences.

When the manava asks the Being what he can do to get him fulfilment of his search for abundance, the Being again elaborates: Open yourself, expand your consciousness to others.

And then it is the danava's turn to ask, "How can I conquer my negative emotional brain circuits?" And the Being replies: "Victory over the negative emotional brain circuits requires the building of positive emotional brain circuits". Use your gift of situational creativity. Explore power but in conjunction with love and goodness.

Finally, the deva. She asks, "Pleasure is becoming boring. Moreover, I am fighting the tendency of addiction. How can I get back in track in my search for happiness?"

The Being says: Explore the archetype of Wholeness. Pleasure-seeking puts too much emphasis on "me." Tends to make you simple hierarchical. Embodying Wholeness requires the practice of tangled hierarchy. Pay attention to the other. Respect the other. It will change the nature of your pleasure. It is worth it.

Combine all the answers, pay attention to the first letter of each and you will find LOVE. Inclusive love - Wholeness - is the modern answer to the human predicament. What is in the quantum worldview that enables us to engage in these four steps of the acronym of LOVE?

The answers are: internality, nonlocality, discontinuity, and tangled hierarchy. And yes; by engaging them we do integrate the human condition. In this way the original story in the Upanishad is vindicated as well.

Internality is the signature of a quantum experience. The external world of our experience, by the necessity of manifestation, is approximately Newtonian and deterministic, detached from the causal world of choice. We have to look to our internal experiences, the subtle world, to find our way back from the physical machine aspect to the causal creative aspect of ourselves.

Nonlocality is signal-less instant communication. Behold! Instant communication means communicating with your self, oneness. The quantum worldview says we human beings have the potentiality of being one with everybody else using this nonlocal communication. Naturally cultivating nonlocality will help shift your me-centeredness towards the universal quantum self.

In the brain, your me-centeredness expresses itself as activities in the brain areas that neuroscientists identify as belonging to the self-agency. The reinforced memories of ego-persona that feed your "me" are stored in these areas. In the body your self-centeredness expresses yourself as vitality tied up to the navel chakra - the welfare of you and you alone. Narcissism. Or for women, in the heart chakra. Too much neediness, needing another to attach to.

Practices like giving, giving unconditionally, obviously take you away from the thoughts of the me-personas. It also raises the energy from your navel chakra to your heart chakra. Giving is just one practice; another practice you can do is the practice of not taking yourself so seriously - Humility. Still another one is Forgiveness. All these practices also help one gain self-respect instead of self-indulgence.

In the quantum worldview, movement can be continuous which is familiar to you, right? Moving cars, moving ants, all move continuously in your experience. The physicist Niels Bohr discovered in 1913 that when electrons jump from one atomic orbit to another, they jump discontinuously, without going through the intermediate space. Such a quantum leap is allowed in the quantum worldview. It is via these quantum leaps of thoughts and feelings that you learn to make positive emotional brain circuits to balance negativity.

The danava in us has to engage what we call *situational creativity*. This is creativity within a fixed archetypal context given by somebody else - a teacher, a good book, a workshop, what have you. It is about finding new meaning and feeling associated with the archetype, within that given archetypal context, new meaning and feeling that you manifest in your living.

Say you are exploring compassion within the context that Jesus gives: love your neighbour. Your neighbour is a lonely old man, and you invite him to dinner. Old stuff will come up: what's in it for me? Will this fellow reciprocate the dinner? Suppose he is boring, but expects to be invited back? It is this old pattern of thinking, your old character that you are trying to replace with a more compassionate character. Proceed. Work on opening your heart and search for new meanings for what comes up.

The creative process is *do-be-do-be-do*. Do is what I described in the previous paragraph. But being is hard for the danava in us - hyperactivity keeps us at bay from being. The tendency is to *do-do-do*. To make room for "be", you engage with concentration meditation, focusing on an object. This slows you down (fig. 9), between thoughts you will now have gaps.

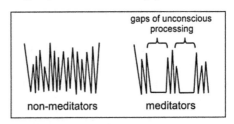

Fig. 9. Meditation slows you down from (a) fast thinking to (b) slowthinking

I always get in a kick on the London Metro; whenever the train comes to a stop, the loudspeaker warns, Mind the gap. That is what you do. You mind the gap between thoughts. The more you mind the gap, the more extended the gap gets. Where do you go when there is a gap in thought? In the unconscious of course. Giving you your much needed unconscious processing. The unconscious is much better at sorting out the new from all the potentialities you have created through your conscious processing, especially when they get a chance of expanding using your be-time.

Now, tangled hierarchy. When you relate to an "other" with pleasure-seeking in mind, you objectify your other. You are the head honcho of the relationship; the other's job is to please you. To make a tangled hierarchy which is a circular relationship, you need to discover the otherness of the other and respect that otherness.

Restraining pleasure is a big help. There is also another problem. The creative mode of the deva in us is fundamental creativity. And the creative process is the same *do-be-do- be-do*. In the *be*-phase, we relax in the waking state to give unconscious processing a chance. During relaxation, the brain's tendency, and fMRI studies prove this, is to go back to the command of what they call *self-agency* and what we call the *ego-character-persona*. The old ego-habits such an engagement with rational intellectualism or information processing to avoid boredom comes back. It is this tendency that the deva has to avoid.

The brain, neuroscientists find, is very predictable. You have a task, it will be in the attention mode; you relax, the brain returns to the occupation with the ego-character-persona, the self-agency.

The quantum solution is: *tangled hierarchy*. We turn to the quantum tangled hierarchical self. How? Through watching our boredom, our intellect and pleasure-seeking mind, but passively without interfering. This witnessing, Buddhists call it *mindfulness*, takes us away from the self- agency towards the quantum self.

Looking inward helps us regain our humanness, the ability of having experience at all. We establish nonlocality for the manava in our lives mainly through the practice of meditation with others; we need community for that. We learn to take discontinuous quantum leaps via situational creativity. And we explore tangled hierarchy via relationships with others and eventually via flow-relationship between the two poles of our own self.

We are potentially one. The big question is, can we experience this unity in our own being, can we experience the nonlocality of our quantum self? How do we even try?

Heart Centering, Non-locality, and Opening to the Quantum Self

Meditation is much more than sitting with your eyes closed and having your mind wandering. Actually, meditation is a gateway towards the innermost core of our being, a way to "experience" and modulate every aspect of our inner world. This is a simple exercise that I (Valentina) use to begin my courses.

Let's prepare for an exercise and sincerely look for the inner guidance and wisdom of your heart. Find a quiet place or prepare for this experience beforehand with a beautiful and harmonious, heart opening music. Close your eyes, sit on a chair or in a meditative pose, with the back straight; relax as deeply as possible, breath slow. For a few moments simply witness your breathing, the air flow, in and out. Allow as much time as you need for each of the following stages. Start with placing your hands on your chest and slowly move your entire attention, in a relaxed manner, at this level. After 2-3 min, you might already perceive a gradual sensation of warmth or vibrations in the area of your chest.

Visualise now a sphere made of luminous white bright light that gradually irradiates from your heart, the middle of your chest area, and allow all your being to relax and expand in all directions. Open to experience a natural state of unconditional love and compassion which is overflowing through all your being. Become aware that this luminous sphere was there since eternity, in your heart, as the divine essence of your soul (the representations of the supramental archetypes that you make with your creative feelings and thinking).

Listen while being more and more relaxed to the silent voice of your heart, identifying deeply with its elevating expansion. Become aware how starting from this level, your aura begins to purify and raise its vitality level, helping you transform, blossom, and even learn your life's lessons.

Do this for as long as you feel comfortable with it. In the end, take a few breaths and come back gradually to your daily activities. You can do this short meditation whenever you want to reconnect to your unity self.

Chapter 5

The Purposive Needs of Consciousness

We are now in the mental age of evolution. With the biological evolution of the neocortical brain, mind could be mapped and ever since we have been evolving in the exploration of the mind, in the exploration of meaning. What does this involve?

The exploration of meaning requires both situational and fundamental creativity. Fundamental creativity gifts us with new archetypal contexts for meaning exploration; situational creativity is our vehicle to explore further these discovered contexts in accordance with societal and personal needs. This then is the first evolutionary need of the mental age.

Evolution requires that meaning exploration must spread to as many members of the human species as possible, if not all, in order for further evolution to take place. This means that not only must we make sure of our personal creativity in the exploration of meaning but also we must make sure of everyone's access to meaning processing and mental creativity. This gives a new dimension to ethics, doesn't it?

The philosopher Ken Wilber has pointed out one other important thing. At every stage of human development, says Wilber, the previous stage must be integrated. As with development, so with evolution. The current mental age of evolution of the rational mind must integrate the evolution of the previous age of the vital mind. This translates into the integration of the processing of feeling and the processing of meaning. It requires inner creativity.

The human species has passed just in few thousands of years through a prodigious process of cultural and psycho-social evolution. This evolution has been limited by a certain epigenetic heritage, the negative emotional brain circuits that affect the brain mechanisms overall to produce counter evolutionary behaviour.

On the other hand, Teilhard de Cardin, a mystic/ scientist, has anticipated the possibility that all human consciousness connects and unites through mental meaning into a whole, that he called "noosphere". However, we cannot correlate into nonlocal unity engaging information processing or engaging our negativity. We can correlate only when we engage with new meaning and positive feelings.

We can see why the balancing and integrating the emotions is necessary. Without giving up negative emotions in favour of positivity towards others, how do we ever help others to progress towards fulfilment in meaning processing?

Many thoughtful people today recognise that there is a crisis in our society. Crisis is danger to most people and the media focuses on this aspect. Connoisseurs know that crisis is also opportunity to make big changes. The time has come to make the evolutionary change from the rational mind to the intuitive mind. This will require the use of inner fundamental creativity and the exploration and embodiment of the archetypes, especially Wholeness.

The results of the Maharishi University research show crime can be reduced if meditators meditate en masse in a city. These results may be controversial, but they are indicative of the power of nonlocal attempts to change towards positivity. Clearly, there is the possibility to heal the entire humanity and to regenerate and re- enchant, through meditation and prayer, the ambience on Earth. It is necessary that an increasing number of people mobilise and start meditation and transformation in unison towards this purpose. We are already doing this in our quantum activism movement. This is being done also by other groups, such as the one initiated by the Heart Math institute, called the *Global Coherence Initiative*. This one aims to mobilise people worldwide, focusing on various zone-specific problems, such as the Tahiti crisis or difficulties caused by a tsunami and so on.

In summary, the current materialist beliefs of our society have stalled evolution. Below I will take these four evolutionary needs one by one to sort out what the problems are in order to get an inkling of where the solutions might be: 1) Movement from Information to Meaning; 2) Emotional Intelligence; 3) Moderation on Pleasure; 4) Evolutionary Ethics.

One final comment in passing. There are only two choices for each of us as far as the movement of consciousness is concerned. We can align ourselves with it or not. And the rule is simple. If you are awake to meaning and purpose, then you can align your movement with the movement of consciousness which is a kind of resonance, and you must if you want to be happy. That is the intelligent thing to do.

From Information to Meaning

Some politicians love the information age; they think it's a huge progress. They believe that processing information in such large scale as we are capable of today (and it is getting even better, right?) is the ultimate in our achievement and therefore, information age is the golden age of our civilisation. This is a very myopic view of the human potential.

What is information? If you don't have any information about the answers to a problem, then all possible answers are equally probable. With information, the probabilities of particular answers grow, and your chance of getting the appropriate answer improves. Information is certainly useful. Information per se often is not tantamount to solving the problem at hand.

Neither does information give you satisfaction or make you happy. Sure, it can be exciting to use the e-mail - it is faster and simpler - to communicate extensively around the world. That may help to keep our worrying mind at bay. It is also an occasionally effective medicine to fight boredom via surfing the Internet. Is your worry really gone because you gained information? Is your boredom gone for ever from your extensive exploration for more information? Are your problems solved? Hardly. The worrying mind gets anxious about the next item of worry. Stop net surfing, and the suffering called *boredom* is back again with gusto. The busy mind has to be kept busy or else it will be unsatisfied and unhappy. Before you were bored; now you have attention deficit disorder.

The elites of our society, the pundits in the media, generate their version of meaning all the time. We the people, however, via Internet and social media, use their meaning as information and get influenced by mere opinion of other people, other people's meaning. In this way, the elites manipulate public opinion.

Misinformation has become so much of a problem that the author of the comic strip *Dilbert* at this writing is doing a series of cartoons on it. I give you a sample. One of the office guys confides in the pointy-headed manager, "I don't know enough about climate change to sound smart when people talk about it". The pointy-headed manger replies, "Try doing your own research. That's how I learned that hurricanes are caused by birds." And when the guy says, "Write that down for me," he adds another misinformation, "And did you know polar bears hate snow?"

You've got to notice that these *pundits* are not solving the problems of concern to you either, and get alarmed. You cannot relegate the responsibility of meaning processing to others; if you do, society suffers, you suffer.

Materialists will say that the intelligent use of information surfing is not to avoid boredom, but to amass money that can bring you satisfaction, even happiness. Examine the life of people who have amassed money, those very innovative money managers of Wall Street. Satisfaction comes when you have engaged your mind with something meaningful. And happiness is enjoying a relaxed moment, doing nothing. Are these money managers engaged in meaningful enterprises? Hardly, they are just making money that is a means, not an end. Are the money managers capable of relaxing? No, they are not capable of enjoying life, of being happy. Instead, they try to find solace for their stressful life in pleasure, which is not only a poor substitute for happiness, but also a detriment to happiness, sometimes everybody's happiness, in the long run, no thanks to the brain's addiction circuits. Indeed, the burn-out rate among these money managers is high.

It is not that information processing is bad, or pleasure is bad, just that they are quite limited achievements. Like money, information processing is also a means, not an end of itself. That is why it gets boring after a while anyway. Surely, you can intuit that there must be more to being human than accumulating lots and lots of means. It is like earning the access to a lot of mountain lakes, but never having the mindset to enjoy the water.

Remember the film, *Pretty Woman*? A fellow is lost in the game of information and moneymaking. And who saves him from his self-imposed dungeon? A prostitute. But this is no ordinary prostitute. She is a prostitute who sells her body for money, to make a living, but not her mind; a prostitute who knows the importance of meaning processing and teaches it to her beau for love. (And of course, the pretty woman herself is also stuck in a meaningless profession from which she is also rescued at the end.)

It's not just about avoiding mental suffering or boredom or missing out on satisfaction and happiness. Look around you. There are environmental problems, a by-product of our search for money without paying attention to meaning. We are running out of cheap energy! Violence, terrorism, global warming, overcrowding, health care crisis, economic meltdowns, there are problems galore, and surely you recognise that these problems are not entirely tractable even with the best of information processing.

Take the case of terrorism. After 9/11, it became a preoccupation of our society to analyse the failure of our intelligence machinery, all based on information processing. If we paid even a little attention to meaning, nothing like this would have ever happened. Terrorism has always existed, and often it is not a bad thing when used against tyranny because the goal is to increase the access of meaning processing for more people. Just remember that the freedom fighters of this country during the revolution began as terrorists from the point of view of the British monarchy. Good or bad, the saving grace was that olden-day terrorism was contained, it was a small-scale activity, relatively speaking. Modern terrorism, on the contrary is large scale capable of affecting many (often innocent) lives at once. Modern terrorism is a direct result of the production of modern weapons capable of large-scale destruction and dissemination of those weapons without thinking out the consequences—which is a reduction of people's access to meaning processing. Weapon sales by America and other advanced countries continue unbridled even after terrorism has become a worldwide problem. We have created the modern terrorist by neglecting meaning in preference to money.

It is foreboding that the social, political and economical structure of the world is about to crash. Almost every aspect of our Western way of living is inadequate to fulfil our evolutionary purpose which is manifesting new meaning and effecting new embodiment of the archetypes. Obviously, this cannot go on like that forever. The economic-socio-political-health care-education, even spiritual, crisis grows as days go by. Humanity is starting to wake up and realise that more than ever, a global action to exit this state of chaos is needed. Many people are looking for the most appropriate way of action. Overall, the global situation is so severe that anybody who hears "a call" doesn't need to wait for personal enlightenment, but to act immediately, with enthusiasm and perseverance, in a beneficial way, according to his /her qualities and inner access to potentialities to change by, even if they are not perfect.

There is one more problem with too much development on the information front. Sooner or later, people of dictatorial ambition will see an opportunity to control people's access to information; on the other hand, they will be able to gain access to people's personal information and gain control over them. The scenario that novelist George Orwell predicted in 1984. Can that happen in a democratic country? By some account, it is already happening.

If information processing cannot give us tangible answers to questions of physical and mental health, of environmental pollution, of energy shortage, of violence and deterioration of society, is there another way to proceed that will give us tangible answers? Is the tangible solution to these problems paying attention to meaning processing, so as to make the transition from information into meaning?

Yes, that is the first step. And fortunately, there are already paradigm shifters in some segments of our society who see this and have begun emphasising meaning. In this way, we have begun to see the creative development of alternatives in our sciences, in medicine and health, and in our businesses. This emphasis has to spread to all our other enterprises: economics, politics, religion, and most importantly education. The emphasis on meaning also has to be embraced by all people, otherwise status quo will continue.

The elites have no interest in making real changes in our society. They have their dogmas-liberal or conservative-makes little difference. Both groups want power. They cater to different bases; so to their own base, they appear to be doing ok. You will notice, most of what they do is just talk. We the people have to pay attention: why do the problems persist?

Most importantly, the paradigm shifters have to stop talking about paradigms to come in the future and recognise that a developing scientific paradigm of all our experiences is already here in the form of quantum science and a quantum worldview. Decades ago, the mention of anything nonphysical would raise the spectre of dualism, but quantum worldview has solved the problem of dualism with the experimentally discovered idea of nonlocality. The quantum worldview has legitimised vital feeling and mental meaning; they both are scientific and measurable stuff. Quantum worldview, by giving a new view of evolution that includes purpose, has legitimised the archetypes and their exploration. Quantum worldview has even given us the tool – creativity - to make changes, even radical changes. For the paradigm shifter, the decision is to heed to what the Dalai Lama says, No model of reality can be built without quantum physics.

For you, the reader, the decision would be to use the new paradigm to make needed changes, awake to higher intelligence than machine intelligence, higher intelligence that you deserve. Or lose it all, lose it to the status quo, lose it to the worldview polarisation between science and religion, lose it to elitism that is destroying democracy, capitalism, and liberal education.

Mental Intelligence

What is intelligence? It is the capacity to respond *appropriately* to a given situation. People who developed the IQ (intelligence quotient) test tell us that all our problem-solving capacities are mental-informational in nature; they are logical-rational, algorithmic capacities, and, as such, they are also measurable. The intelligence quotient that IQ tests measure relates to our mental- informational intelligence. Is IQ all there is to mental intelligence?

Looking for differences between the general psycho mental capacity of the common man and the one of a genius, it was found that usually people don't use their brain more than about 5%. We all have been in a situation where there is a delay between what we want to do, the objectives we establish and the facts that are our reality. Most often we cannot hold on to the positive decisions that we make and we fail chronically, and ultimately we lose self-confidence. Then we feel weak, with an intense feeling of guilt. And then, most often the tomorrow presents us, like today, like yesterday, with the same failures, and years pass by without any deep transformation in our being. There are actually ways to practice and strengthen self-control, just like we do with our muscles, as we will describe in the following. Will power is strongly connected with the mental state.

An Exercise for the Amplifying of the Self Control: The Wave Method

There are methods that help us become stronger in will power when practiced regularly. Here is one:

Think intensely of ocean waves that advance towards the shore progressively becoming bigger and bigger as they join together, and break by the shore. We can compare this wave with some food that we crave for, such as French fries. After a few such exercises, you will see that your craving will naturally diminish.

Live fully Now and don't postpone anything for tomorrow. What we don't do today, we will never do. Keep in mind that the self-control and will power are not active in many of us, therefore they need to be trained on a daily basis.

Integrating Information (Old Meaning) and New Meaning

Problem solving for an IQ test is algorithmic; therefore, people who tout rationalism are quite happy with IQ and rational-logical mental intelligence as the only measure of people's intelligence. You can see that IQ really measures little more than machine intelligence, it focuses mostly on the capacity we have for using the mind as a machine. For good IQ, we need to process meaning only in the contexts etched in our memory; contexts given by the elites and manipulators of the society. The bigger storage of memory we have giving us access to a vast repertoire of learned contexts - information- the greater is our IQ. The greater is our reasoning power or algorithmic processing capacity, the greater IQ we have.

It is like the grandmasters of chess that memorise the successful moves in many previous contexts of board positions, thousands of them. Whereas us, ordinary mortals, struggle with figuring out the future effect of a particular move, the grandmaster makes his or her move simply from memory, using only a little reasoning for adapting to the present situation.

Real life is not a chess game played with fixed playthings on a fixed board and with fixed rules. Nor is life a series of IQ tests. The contexts for our meaning processing change constantly and often unpredictably. They may not be big changes of context, but nevertheless just memory processing and situational reasoning will never be enough to find the appropriate response in meaning. You say, let the pundits do it, let our leaders do it. That's how Donald Trump, a pathological liar with dictatorial ambitions, was elected president of America in 2016.

It is not hard to find other meanings to situations than the established meanings. Zen masers, all spiritual teachers of transformation are masters of teaching you that. Suppose a Zen master asks you holding up a marker, "What is it?" And you say, "It is a marker." Now the Zen master says, "I will hit you thirty times." Strange response, but Zen masters are famous for their strangeness. And guess what? If you have never been to a Zen master, it is unlikely that you will even know what the Zen master is trying to say to you! Maybe he is just a sadist.

When I (Amit) was a beginner in Zen tradition and encountered this particular behaviour of a Zen master, I didn't understand it. I just attributed it to quirkiness- everybody knows that Zen masters are quirky, right? Only ten years later, when I was reading John Searle's article on mind and meaning that I understood that the Zen master was trying to draw our attention to the fact that a marker is not only a marker used for writing although that is its most frequent use. A marker can be used also to hit someone (although not very hard). Heck, a marker can even be used as a barometer: if you measure the time of fall of a marker from a given height, you can figure out the atmospheric pressure at that height of the atmosphere.

Therefore, mental intelligence is more than IQ intelligence because mind is more than a machine, more than our remembered responses to previous stimuli.

Who hasn't heard the phrase "street smart?" Or the phrase "the school of hard knocks?" These phrases refer to mental intelligence that responds skilfully and often with originality as opposed to formal IQ intelligence which always follows established wisdom. People who are street smart or have learned from the school of hard knocks don't depend on their memory of formal learning based on artificial simplified contexts. They look at real life contexts just as they are- always a new context that requires a new response. In other words, creativity.

Remember this: mental information processing always takes place within given contexts of thinking. If the problem you are looking at requires a brand-new context, you are stuck, there is no amount of information thinking or net surfing that is of help.

An intelligent human being has what is called "cognitive reservoir", a kind of "spare wheel of the cerebral possibilities". To enrich this cognitive reservoir, to enrich our abilities and to awaken latent capacities, it is necessary to engage in intellectual activities, such as reading or studying, in those domains that make us passionate; also to practice methods of focus for improving memory.

Our brain is the most important physical interface of consciousness, an instrument through which are controlled much of the processes that take place inside our body. It contains about 1 billion neurons. The brain, together with the organs of the heart chakra, is the most important organ in the body and it influences the quality of our life in a major way. Brain has neuroplasticity. By strengthening the cerebral performances via processing of new meaning, we develop a tonic, lucid, structured brain-mind, a good memory and repertoire of learned skills, and focusing capacity. Just like an athlete doesn't work over one type of muscles only in order to feel in great shape, but over the whole body, it is not enough to eat healthy, or to breath pure air, but we must as well train in mental focus and breathing, meditative techniques, such as the ones offered in yoga.

Einstein was not an information fancier. Some teacher once asked him in a test situation, "What is the speed of sound?" Einstein had said, "I don't clutter my brain with details like that." Nobody I think ever measured his IQ, but it may not have been very high judging from the selective nature of his childhood educational prowess-good in physics, music, and math, but not in much else. Dr. Diamond actually examined a portion of Einstein's brain. As expected, she discovered a large number of glial cells in the left parietal lobe, a kind of neurological formation, described as "an association zone for other association zones of the brain". The glial cells act as a liaison that keeps together the nerve cells, and help in transmitting electrochemical signals between neurons, in other words, synaptic transmission involved in new meaning processing.

What is the lesson from all this? To integrate new meaning in our being is to be elevated from machine mental intelligence to real mental intelligence, that is, the capacity to take an occasional quantum leap of meaning.

This is only a first step. Creativity directed to a product in the outer arena of the world is outer creativity; important but is not enough. Evolution demands more. There is one more step. Loosely speaking, it is the step of paying attention to our inner life, to direct our exploration in such a way as to establish meaning in the center of our being.

We pay attention to the interface of the outer and the inner. We pay attention to events of synchronicity - outer events that reverberate with inner meaning - to assume more importance and become signposts of where life should take us.

When we engage in creativity while paying attention to the play of synchronicity in our lives, the unfolding of meaning becomes more obvious, clearly amplified.

We begin paying attention to dreams, the ongoing unfolding of our life in the realm of meaning. Everyone knows that what is intense in our waking life affects our dream life. Similarly, we allow the intensity in our dream life affect our waking life.

The thought comes sooner or later- can we direct our creativity to change the director of our inner processing? Instead of the mental ego directing our inner life, can we let the higher power of God/quantum self to direct our inner theatre? Not just during the episodes of some outer creativity projects, but on a more regular basis. Thus begins the journey of inner creativity by taking quantum leaps to change our inner life.

Very soon we become aware of a difficulty. Our emotions create problems with changing our inner life to make meaning its center point. So, we begin to pay attention to our feelings, our emotional life.

And this is good; this is an essential part of our evolutionary need. Don't forget. Evolution requires that inner creativity not only becomes a going thing for me,but for all humanity. To assure that I need to open my heart to everyone in my local interaction sphere and give each a helping hand towards creativity if I can. This requires giving up competition in favour of cooperation, giving up negative feeling in favour of positive feelings towards others. In other words, deal with the danava in all of us. But how to do that?

In the last few centuries, people of wasp cultures, white anglo-saxon protestants have been the most successful in ways that we count success which is dictated by the very same dominating people. The ruling phrase here is competition and domination. It is hard for people of this mindset to change to a cooperation-based society. If we are looking for and waiting for them to change, we are wasting our time. This movement has got to start outside the wasp cultures, perhaps in the developing countries called *the second world*, the BRICS countries - Brazil, Russia, India, China, and South Africa, although I am doubtful about China, which is too totalitarian at the moment. Instead of China, probably Eastern and Southern Europe - countries like Portugal, Italy, Romania, Czech Republic - may be our better hopes.

And don't think we are proposing exclusion of the WASP cultures; exploring Wholeness is inclusion. We will keep trying and cater to the small number of interested people in these cultures. Maybe after we have introduced transformation elsewhere and demonstrated that it works, the WASP cultures will catch on; once that happens, they will even be better at it than the rest of the world.

Methods for Cerebral Training and for Increasing Neural Connections

Many of my (Valentina's) students and patients prove to be so caught in their daily routine and stereotypical behaviours that they don't even notice the challenges and opportunities around them. To begin the cerebral training, i recommend that they do for a certain period of time, eight methods, each of them dynamizing a certain area of the brain. You can also try the practice systematically for a week, let's say, and note down daily what you notice. Then you can continue for longer periods of time.

1. Let's use the limbs of the body in a different way than we are used to. For example, 1) brush your hair or teeth, mix food or do any other simple activities with the other hand than the one you are used to. 2) Close your eyes and "feel' the way you need to pass in a room. 3) Become aware of

the sounds and smells around you. 4) Use the foot (instead of hand) to open a door or to lift an object off the floor. 5) Read a page in a book upside-down.

2. When you have the tendency to criticise someone, address him or her, on the contrary, and give a compliment! By thus putting at bay few of the prejudices you have over this person, you will start acknowledging that this person has simply different points of view than yourself.

3. Take a quick but attentive look inside the fridge, then close the fridge door, and enumerate the food products that you saw. Do the same with a room, a painting or the view from a window.

4. For five minutes daily, project yourself as another person, and contemplate certain actions or events from his/her perspective. Let go preconceived ideas about that person. As if you are an actor interpreting a role and playing it, intuiting his thoughts, states, emotions and feelings.

5. Breathe ten minutes daily as consciously as possible, directing the energy of the breathing towards the heart.

6. At each hour on the hour, try to remember what you did the last sixty minutes. Even done for a few seconds, this exercise helps you to become more attentive. At the end of the day, make a quick synthesis of the events in the day. When you notice empty memories, it is for those events for which you were more or less unaware of what you did. An advanced exercise is to re-memorise the day starting from the end to the beginning.

7. In order to develop flexibility and adaptability, do something different every day. For example, shop for your food in another shop than the one you are used to. Choose another way back home rather than the usual one. Bake a cake for no special reason. Engage in a new sport. Meet a new neighbour. Doing the same actions every day leads to a stasis of the brain. Diverse stimulation is one of the keys of cerebral developing.

8. Keep the back as straight as possible most of the time. You can imagine, for example, when you walk, that you have on your head a bunch of books that you need to keep in balance. The effect will be quite rapid. Such a bodily attitude creates the inner attitude of self control and control over situations.

Integrating Meaning and Feeling, Negative and Positive Emotions

Is there intelligence aside from IQ intelligence and mental intelligence that integrate information and new meaning? In the West, some people have long recognised the fashionableness in the culture to suppress emotions. We, men specially, are taught to suppress emotions because when emotions cloud our psyche, mind and mental logic cannot function very well, and even the best IQ is not of much help. Only by suppressing emotions, can we retain control, can we use our high IQ to its fullest extent to succeed in life, or so we are told. The problem with this approach is that if we become emotion suppressors we suppress all emotions. We not only suppress those negative emotions such as anger, which are detrimental to appropriate action that demands reason but also tend to suppress positive emotions (such as love) that we covet, that we intuit add to the quality of life and the very ability to intuit. What kind of intelligence is that that reduces the quality of life instead of enhancing it?

If you like science fiction, you can see the ongoing theme of the famous Star Trek shows here: reason vs. emotion. Reason is efficient, reason enables you to better function in a crunch, but without emotion isn't the reason to live compromised? Doesn't reason become "dry" and mundane when there is no passion in it?

In recent years, there is much talk about emotional intelligence - intelligence that enables you to appropriately respond to emotions. Emotional intelligence is a funny beast.

Suppose there is anger in your environment and you are caught up in it. Yet you are not suppressing it. If you also express your anger as everybody else in the environment, wouldn't the situation only get worse?

So you neither express nor suppress, what happens? Have you done it? If you have, very soon you discover, it takes a great deal of effort and a disciplined practice. People of very limited commitment to exert effort and discipline would succumb to either suppression (in the West and North) or expression (in the East and South).

The idea of disciplined practices for achieving emotional intelligence has made into the psychology literature. Let's look at the practices espoused in a popular book by the psychologist Daniel Goleman, *Emotional Intelligence:*

1. awareness of one's own emotional nature;

2. emotion management;

3. controlling emotions in the service of goal-oriented motivation;

4. empathy (the ability to share other people's emotions without losing one's objectivity);

5. handling emotionally intimate relationships.

Awareness or mindfulness training makes you aware what your emotional habits are, whether you express or suppress, how you emotionally interact with others, etc. Awareness practice also enables you to react to emotion without suppressing or expressing, but just meditating on it, at least to a limited extent. Emotion management is prioritising, when to express and when to suppress, and when to do your best to do neither, that is, meditate. Controlling emotions (namely suppressing it) when your job calls for it is the civilised compromise that every professional is forced into. The practice is to suppress as consciously as one can.

Empathy training is something every psychotherapist attempts to have, but as they very well know it is a tricky practice. And you know what? Practice helps, but it never makes it to perfection. This is the reason that therapists burn out.

What empathy training entails is the ability to be in other person's shoes, the person who is suffering from emotional outburst. Psychologists think they have a pretty good idea of how the mind works. Especially if you learn to pick up nonverbal cues – neuro-linguistic programming of people- you can form a pretty good theory of the other's mind, and feign empathy. But is it the real thing?

I (Amit) have been researching this subject for a long time, ever since I had a discussion with the yoga psychologist Uma Krishnamurthy on this subject at a conference in Bangalore, India. I had brought a group from America to the conference and Uma and I both were speakers. We both attended a small meeting in which some people of our group were sharing their feelings and it went a little out of hand. In other words, I didn't do very well as a group leader in keeping emotions under control. So Uma taught me about the conceptual difference between sympathy and empathy. I myself had become sympathetic with the group members, she said. Like them, I, too, had wallowed in negative emotions. Instead, I realised, I have to learn to relate with empathy—the capacity to feel other's emotions without losing one's objectivity.

Long practice on developing empathy has taught me one thing. Practice just cannot make you transform to an empathic being; in difficult situation, sympathy always breaks through and you pick up suffering from the person you are trying to help. What good does that do? Before there was one person suffering, now there are two. In those situations, you have to stay with the problem until you have taken a quantum leap to objectivity. Please note that even the quantum leap does not permanently transform you into an empathic! It just enables you to see through a particular situation.

We now know that the sympathy reaction is due to our brain's mirror neurons that mimic the other's behaviour. It is local communication. Empathy on the other hand requires a quantum leap to connect to the other nonlocally.

Master Ryokan, a wise man in the community, was not into preaching or judging people or reprimanding. His brother's son became delinquent, and naturally the father turned to his wise brother for help. Ryokan came but contrary to his brother's expectation he said not a word of admonition. However, he stayed overnight. In the morning as he was ready to leave and as his belligerent nephew was helping him to tie his shoelace, he felt a warm drop of water falling on his shoulders. He looked up straight into Ryokan's eyes which were full of tears. Ryokan returned home but the boy changed his ways. This is empathy and how it works.

The last item of the list above, to partake in intimate emotional relationship is the ultimate practice that takes you beyond ordinary emotional intelligence. This subject is an important aspect of the transformational practice, so I devote part of an entire chapter to it. See later.

If you have tried to deal with emotions in an intimate relationship, then you know one thing. You cannot resolve an emotional conflict at an intimate level without paying attention to the present context. No previous learning will do. In other words, you will need to pay attention to intuitions, take quantum leaps of creativity on a regular basis, to maintain an emotional intimate relationship.

People who look at emotions in a brain-based way, that is, assume that emotions are solely brain phenomena, also assume (wrongly) that the brain can be trained to learn all the five aspects of emotional intelligence mentioned above. The brain has five times more built in negativity than it has positivity. In this way, brain rewiring would not be much effective using only the brain to invoke positivity. Fortunately, in a consciousness-based science, emotions are only secondarily brain-based (the brain circuits); primarily, they are psychological effects of feelings that arise in the vital body connections of the physical organs at the chakras. These psychological effects of feelings have two sources. First, mind gives meaning to feelings and in the process "mentalises" them producing unwanted emotional software. Second, feelings have correlated physiological effects that, by affecting the representation maker, the brain, also affects the mind, that which is represented in the brain. Physiology affects psychology.

The mentalisation of feelings unfortunately is tricky and often we interpret feelings wrongly. In those cases, the solution is to invite the supramental to see the problem correctly, hence again the need for quantum leaps.

Emotional intelligence practiced with the inclusion of occasional quantum leaps is what is required to satisfy the evolutionary need of integrating meaning and feeling. When we involve the supramental to explore archetypes such as Love or Goodness, the higher chakras open further, the navel chakra and above and new positive feelings come into play. Giving appropriate meanings to those as guided by the archetypal exploration helps build positive emotional brain circuits and this offers us a much more effective strategy for attaining emotional intelligence.

Emotional Education

"Emotions are an intimate part of our life and are the bricks from which we build the activity of our Soul", as meditation teacher Swami Advaitananda emphasises. The silent, mysterious presence of emotions in our daily existence causes them to be ignored or sometimes even denied their right to be a part of our daily existence even though thoughts get so much attention, and yet have the same immaterial nature. I (Valentina) learnt from him about values such as straightforwardness, purity, patience and perseverance. Later on, Amit showed me further the healing and integrative value of kindness, tolerance and acceptance.

Our emotions mark a major difference between a robotic mind and an intuitive and spontaneous mind (according to the level of understanding about the way emotions function). In most educational systems today, the emphasis is placed on logic and memory, the two components of the "robotic self ", the main constituents of our auto-pilot. This kind of education weakens the activity of the soul and cuts us off from the reality of our emotions. Even in situations when students are encouraged to discover and train the intuitive part of their mind, the emotional part is little, if at all engaged.

An important observation we can easily make is that most of the decisions we take in life are dictated by our emotions in that moment, and not by our logic or previously accumulated experiences. This shows once again the paramount importance of emotional education and control since this largely influences our future decisions, therefore our future in general. Our memory works better when feelings are involved. This is of great use to me (Valentina) in my sessions, noticing how the mind only makes associations between notions that are correlated with corresponding feelings. Recent studies have shown that the quality of our emotions influences the capacity to memorise them. An act that was supported by strong emotions will have a strong imprint in our memory and will be more easily accessible than an act that does not trigger any emotion in us.

Neuroscience is thus confirming now that what spiritual traditions have maintained for thousands of years: "what you love is what you will sooner or later become." In this statement we recognise the formative power of one of the strongest emotion generators that we have in our life: LOVE. We don't become what we consider correct, we don't become what we consider right or wrong. We don't become what we think but that what we think with LOVE, what we emotionally seek through love.

In the process of learning we frequently use this associative mechanism between feeling and thought but more or less unconsciously. Through the intense "training" of the associative power of our consciousness that we go through today, we obtain an almost instantaneous process of association – the connection between an action and the emotion that is predominant in our inner medium at the time we perform that action. In this way the memories that are created depend not on the quality of information that we get but on the emotion that takes place at the time of receiving the information.

As the meditation teacher genially points out, "to make a complete analogy about the relationship between the information-processing mind and the emotions (feeling and meaning) we can say that the information processor mind is the librarian that is taking care of a large library. The emotions are the content of all the books that are in that library. The librarian is not the author of the books but is rather keeping them in good order, thus making their content accessible in our daily life. The intense cultivation of the activity of the librarian makes the library develop the way the books are arranged on the shelves and the different systems of access to the information."

Yet, we should not forget that having good informational schemes only makes the arrangement of the books better, but it will not change the content of the books. We often ignore this aspect and we train only the librarian. This is why we experience richness in mental informational schemes, but poverty in the experiences that "populate" our mental schemes. The library is neatly organised, but contains only a few books. Furthermore, we repeatedly read the same books and every time we want something more we only try to rearrange the books on the shelves in another way.

Today, since the environment is suppressing the emotional manifestations, most teenagers grow emotionally retarded with severe consequences on the learning process. Lots of kids diagnosed in a hurry (and with the usual superficiality of the health care system that I (Valentina) meet almost in every country) with ADHD, PTSD, and then they are immediately put on a medication that will only further destroy their brain and association capacity. Moreover, young children chaotically associate the notions they learn at school with the emotions they experience in their family or with their colleagues, or with the adventures they have in the constant attempt to discover the world. From this blend of emotions, half suppressed and half uncontrolled they build the content of their future "library". Then, no matter how smart they might become, they cannot pass a certain level of conscious development because they have a poor library of life experiences. What we ignore is the fact that in this way most of the knowledge students learn in school is structured around chaotic emotions that are not making the things move better; on the contrary it is removing a lot of information from being efficiently accessible in their daily existence.

Therefore, there is a clear need to start developing a coherent system of emotional education. Even the very notion of emotional education will be enriched with a new meaning from this perspective. It is important not only for the sake of our future generations, but for the sake of the human civilisation itself and represents one of the crucial entrance requirement for the next stage in its evolution.

Moderation of Pleasure

In chapter 4, we talked about our *deva* problem – uncontrolled pleasure - a problem that not only leads to addiction but also ruins relationships because you are using the other for your own selfish interest.

Scientific materialism leads to a permissive society with disastrous consequences. Religions, even the wisdom traditions went the other way. They insisted that people give up entirely on pleasure. The solution is in the middle: moderation.

You probably know this story in Buddha's life. At a crucial point of his spiritual journey, Buddha was worried about his own situation. Huge restraints on pleasure had not produced any return whatsoever; instead he was enervated both in body and mind. Then he saw a musical string instrument and a quantum leap took place in his psyche. If you are too lax on the tension of the strings, no musical notes come out; but you make the tension too strong, the strings break. So his quantum leap insight was: the middle path, moderation.

This is part of the solution. Learning about the brain's pleasure circuits tells us that the pleasure circuits have much to do with reward. If one is to refrain from pleasure, then he or she must be given a reward, some other pleasure item. The overall dynamic does not change.

Quantum science, through its emphasis on vital energy dynamics has a slightly different solution. Enjoy pleasure, but differently. The pleasure is in the brain but of course your body organs are also involved. What happens if you not only enjoy the pleasure but also pay attention to the organs in the body that are involved?

For example, you are eating good food; your brain is producing pleasure molecules with gusto. Gobble, gobble, gobble. The faster you eat, the more intense is the pleasure. Often this leads to overeating and later discomfort. Pleasure ends up in some pain. Not so good. If you pay attention to your navel area where your digestive organs are, this will slow you down. Eat slow. At the end of your meal you will notice two things: 1) you are able to stop your food intake right when you are satisfied; overeating will stop. And 2) as your slowness continues after the meal is finished you will discover happiness, a kind of relaxation. Where is it coming from? From the expansion of consciousness. This is a transformative reward. This is what moderation practiced in the quantum way is about. Gradually, you learn to replace some of the pleasure aspect of your account by happiness in the form of the expansion of consciousness.

Consider the other source of intense pleasure in humans—sex (in happy cases: lovemaking). People talk about the joy of sex; it is all in the brain. Fast, fast, fast; lots of oxytocin and dopamine molecules. Usually, it is roughly about a seven minute affair ending with an orgasm for the male. The female would have to be lucky to achieve an orgasm, too. And after the orgasm with ejaculation, the male turns over and goes to sleep.

The female stays awake with some lack of satisfaction - to put it mildly.

Change this dynamic to slow lovemaking – meaning you emphasise on love, which, together with slow movements, may give you the chance to collapse the intense sexual drive into heart energy; you are also paying attention to your breathing. The pleasure may reduce in intensity, but will be adequate. And what will reduce is your tendency to turn over and go to sleep. And if you respond to your partner's desire to cuddle you will discover with surprise an unmistakable happiness coming over you. Why? Your consciousness is expanding, becoming inclusive, inclusive of your partner, a feeling we all call Love.

We have mentioned the chakras before. There are selves in the body at the navel and at the heart level. There are two chakras lower in the body, below the navel level; one at the base of the spine (anus) called the *root chakra* (in sanskrit *muladhara*), the other at the sex organs, called the *sex chakra* (in sanskrit *swadhisthana*). There are potentialities of vital movement at these chakras, but they cannot collapse in the absence of a self. If we pay attention to the body and we even orient these vital movements at will, upwards, these energies have a chance to collapse, moving up to the higher chakras with self. Note: *collapsing* is the term we are suggesting for the processes of transmutation and sublimation which are mentioned in tantra.

There are two choices, 1) the energy is collapsed at the navel chakra. This is what happens in our fast mode of pleasure seeking when we are paying scant attention to the body. The navel chakra by itself is selfish; collapsing energy there makes us narcissistic. 2) The energy is collapsed at the heart chakra. Heart chakra is the chakra of love, our doorway to selflessness and expansion of consciousness. This is what we promote when we adapt a slow lifestyle.

The New Evolutionary Ethics

Traditionally, in the East, social ethics are largely ignored; ethics are practiced rigorously only as a preparation for the spiritual journey. In the West, the material advantage of social ethics was recognised early on, but too much materialism, now scientioically rationalised, has eroded its practice considerably. Most of us suffer from severe ambiguous feelings as far as ethics are concerned because, according to materialist science, the scope of ethics is very limited.

Biologists, the neo-Darwinists have invented a form of scientific ethics based on biology in the form of a metaphysical principle called *genetic determinism*. The idea is that our behaviour is entirely determined by our genes, we are gene machines. Our mind, consciousness, and macro behaviour, all have one ultimate purpose, to perpetuate our genes, to guarantee the survival of our genes. It follows from this perspective that we should have some interest beyond selfishness, some natural tendencies of selfless altruistic behaviour.

For example, if I have some genes common with you, I am helping my own genetic propagation and survival by taking care of you. Hence, I behave altruistically towards you depending on how much genetic commonality I have with you.

This would be a nice theory because if it were correct, this kind of bio ethics would have been compulsory- our genes would have made sure of that. Unfortunately, the empirical data on altruism just does not conform to this theory. When altruistic people see someone in a calamity, they offer help irrespective of any genetic connection whatever, for example to even a foreigner.

There is also the question of how you handle the good-evil dichotomy built in our collective unconscious. In the olden days, evil was recognised as an entity - Devil- opposed to God; siding with it was a sure indication that after you die you will go to devil's abode called *hell*. The fear of hell or desire of heaven was an incentive to follow ethics. But who do you know nowadays that takes heaven and hell that seriously anymore only to sacrifice selfishness, especially when there is ambiguity?

Ethics and values are important even today to enough people, enough to make a difference in the 2018 midterm elections in the USA. The reason so many of us, even today, have a conscience to think ethically in the face of so much growing unethical behaviour in our societies is embedded in the collective unconscious. The problem is, negative emotional brain circuits are built in; so we respond with negative emotion to suitable stimuli naturally, without effort. It is not so with positive emotions, few of us have them - good karma from past life. Only if we have them, can we respond to the calling of the "good" in the collective unconscious.

Religions, of course, universally have supported ethics in various forms ("do good, be good"; do unto others that which you would want others to do unto you; if I am not for myself, who am I? if I am only for myself what am I?). For dualistic and simplistic religions, the rationale is clear - fear of God. This rational is no longer enough; notice how unshakable is the evangelical support for Trump in America.

In quantum scientific terms we can give a better rational for ethics and good-evil distinction. Good is that which takes you towards Wholeness and evil that which takes you away from Wholeness. This may prove to be too ambiguous for specifically those situations where you most need clarity. Also, this base-level ethics may not be proactive enough.

We need a new ethics to live by, no less. Can quantum science give us more directed incentive towards ethical action? It can. It does.

Quantum physics is the physics of possibilities and hints that we, the observer/participant choose out of these possibilities the actual event of our experience. When Fred Alan Wolf coined the phrase "we choose our own reality" based on this hint, his dictum spread like wild fire among new agers. The same thing happened when a recent movie and a book named

The Secret suggested that we manifest things that we intend for us by choosing it and waiting. The idea became very popular among new agers and became the butt of jokes for many comic strips because obviously, the idea is too simplistic.

Previously, we mentioned one subtlety of the choice among quantum possibilities. The consciousness we choose from is not the ego, but a non-ordinary cosmic state of consciousness which traditionalists call God. Only when "my" ego-intention resonates with the movement of cosmic consciousness does my intention become manifest. What is the criterion for the evolutionary movement of consciousness or what in a previous time, people referred to as "God's will?" In other words, on what basis do we choose when we are in that cosmic consciousness/ God? The answer emerges when you consider evolution.

There is an evolutionary movement of consciousness that is going on towards manifesting the supramental archetypes embodied in us. "God's will" is always driving us towards that goal. When we have a creative encounter with God and a creative insight comes, we have the ultimate ethical choice: shall I use this insight for selfish means or shall I use it for the greater good, for the evolutionary goal of the movement of consciousness? The clearer we are about our ethics, the more appropriate is our action that follows the creative insight. Let's call this *evolutionary ethics*.

Suppose we solidly base our actions on evolutionary ethics, on the very scientific notion of the evolution of consciousness and the demand of evolutionary movement of consciousness upon us that meaning processing, old and new, must be a privilege for everyone. In this way, the active principle of evolutionary ethics becomes this: our actions are ethical when they maximise the evolutionary potential of every human being. Imagine a society where such an ethics is in place, what this will do to our politics, to the practice of law and journalism, the practice of businesses, to the practice of health and healing, to how we educate our children.

This is part and parcel of quantum spirituality, why we emphasise pursuing the archetype of Wholeness rather than the archetype of self. Because, as argued before, pursuing the archetype of self is tantamount to giving up on evolutionary ethics.

Previously we spoke of mental and emotional intelligence. Evolutionary ethics demands that the pursuits of mental and emotional intelligence must be undertaken and achieved by the bulk of the entire human species; future evolution demands it. How do I not only achieve true mental intelligence supplemented by emotional intelligence for myself but also help all my fellow humans achieve the same goal? The new science has some answers, the discussion of which is beyond the scope of this book. Read my upcoming book, *The Ascent of Humanity.*

If it bothers you that some people are able to get away with ethical violations (the investment bankers for example who helped cause the 2007 economic meltdown and still drew huge bonuses or the Trump boondoggles), don't worry. They can get away now, but Captain Karma eventually gets everyone. You have to learn to be ethical, or else you get forever caught up in the birth-death- rebirth cycle and repeated *karmuppance*.

Chapter 6

Setting the Stage for the Transformational Journey

There is now much accumulated empirical evidence in favour of both survival-after-death and reincarnation and additionally, there is a good detailed theory that explains all the data. Read my book, *Physics of the Soul*. The theory and data on reincarnation suggests the pivotal factor in determining our place in the creativity spectrum.

Theoretical considerations based on the new quantum science give us further clarity. Previously, we classified creative acts in two classes- those acts of discovery that we call "fundamental creativity" and the acts of invention that we call "situational creativity". Following the terminology of yoga psychology, let's denote the propensity for fundamental creativity by the Sanskrit word *sattva* and that for situational creativity by another Sanskrit word *rajas*. And then there is also the propensity for no creativity at all, the tendency of exhibiting just conditioning in one's actions. This propensity we will denote by the Sanskrit word *tamas*.

Reincarnational theory suggests that what we mainly bring from our past reincarnations are mental propensities including these three propensities of *sattva, rajas, and tamas.* Now mind you, conditioning is ever present; it is a price we pay for growing up and cluttering our brain with memories. So tamas dominates when we begin our reincarnational journey, only gradually with many incarnations, giving way to creative tendencies of rajas and sattva.

Clearly, our place on the creativity spectrum depends crucially on our bringing with us when we incarnate anew a lot of sattva - the capacity to discover, discovery is the most highly regarded act of creativity. The more sattva we bring, the more is our tendency to delve into fundamental creativity. In the same way, the reincarnational inheritance of rajas determines how successful we can be in the empire-building type of creativity, situational creativity. And how much sattva or rajas we can bring to bear in this life depends on our reincarnational history.

The purpose of our reincarnational journey is to discover the archetypes and embodying them, a job that takes us many lives. This provides us the personal motivation towards creativity - it is the archetypes that motivate us towards creatively discovering them.

In the movie *The Groundhog Day,* the hero is driven by the archetype of love from life to life until he learns love's selfless essence. We all are doing that sort of thing, pursuing one archetype or another. Just like our hero, we remain unconscious of what we are doing when we begin our reincarnational journey to catch on to the game only as we mature.

Archetypes: Remembering Your Dharma

There is one common theme in all the ideas we have mentioned so far; hopefully you have noticed. Healing, giving, nature, relationships, what is the common thread in all of them? The archetypes. Healing is about the archetype of Wholeness; giving is about the archetype of Goodness; nature is about the archetype of Beauty, relationship is about the archetype of Love.

Giving is also about the archetype of Abundance. You give that which you possess in abundance. Money seldom gives you that feeling of abundance; there is never enough. If you are poor in the archetypes of Love, Goodness, and Justice, you cannot give freely.

Human beings have been struggling with the archetype of Power ever since we have any data. The ego's tendency is to amass power because you are the only head honcho you recognise; others are important if somehow they are your extension. You need power to keep these others in tow. In this way, you are using power to empower yourself, it may satisfy your need for domination, but does it satisfy? Are you ready to explore power to empower others?

The ultimate scourge of the materialist society is that we have misconstrued the archetype of Self. In the West, this is recognised in the tradition of alchemy. We have gold in our true self, our true I; we choose copper instead, the I/me of ego at the exclusion of the quantum self. All archetypes are our doorway to alchemical transformation; however, the archetype of Wholeness and self top the list.

"Man cannot live without attachment to some object which transcends and survives him," said the sociologist Emile Durkheim. Archetypes are those objects. They are so dear to us that whenever we die and reincarnate, we choose an archetype to explore in the next life. We select a portion of our accumulated karma suited for that archetype, our dharma.

If we follow our dharma, we are satisfied and happy. If you are not satisfied with your profession, it is time to reexamine your archetype of pursuit. May be there is a mismatch.

How do you find your archetype? They come to us via crystallisation experiences as the Wholeness archetype came to me back in 1973. Many creative people have similar experiences.

They also come to us via dreams. Dreams are full of symbology; if you learn to look beyond the symbology, they will lead you to your archetype. Or you can analyse your dreams with a teacher.

Other ways of finding you archetype is via astrology and the recently rediscovered enneagram system. There are nine enneagrams corresponding to the nine major archetypes above. Enneagrams reflect your personality which may be sabotaging you from knowing your archetype and keeping you from your spiritual journey. Being aware of your personality helps to discover your enneagram and give away the secret of your archetype.

By the same token, your character traits that you brought and activated in this life are also an indicator of your chosen dharma. If you regress yourself to your childhood via a memory exercise, you may find character traits that existed then and are indicative of what you came endowed with, but life played a trick on you.

Integrating Thinking and Living: Walking Your Talk

Creative insights in the outer arena require a lot of hard work to manifest into a product. It is a fact that many people enjoy the creative process, have the insights, but cannot master the effort needed to finish the product. Only because of all the goodies (the carrots of behavioural psychology) that may come one's way, this laziness in manifesting never reaches epidemic proportions.

In inner creativity, however, the manifestation stage is even harder than outer creativity, if anything. The behavioural rewards, the goodies are not public, but private. Because of this double-whammy, many more people stop their creative process at the level of the insight; they never try much to live their insight.

What is worse is that the prevalent materialist culture in a subtle way invades the mind-set of the inner creative.

The inner creative falls for what Chogyam Trungpa Rinpoche used to call spiritual materialism and starts teaching what she knows from quantum leaps but has not manifested in being. She becomes caught with the expectations of the same rewards that drive outer creativity- name, fame, power, money, sex, outer accomplishments, etc. (Alas! The Trungpa himself was not entirely exempt from the same mind-set.)

Some transpersonal thinkers (for example, read Wilber's books) complicate the situation further by introducing a certain glamour and mystique about the "superconscious" states one achieves with the quantum leaps by classifying them with philosophical sophistry. This kind of classification has no scientific basis and moreover, the bottom line does not change. Without carrying through the manifestation stage, no permanent transformation takes place from any quantum leap, however exalted classification you give to it.

This overemphasis on the mere superconscious experience will not do for quantum spirituality. We must break this tendency to be lazy at the most crucial point of our personal development and manifest in our being every supramental insight we have.

Fortunately, thanks to positive psychology, a scientific classification is now available in the form of the scale of happiness (fig. 2). We can make a similar scale of intelligence (fig. 10). And of course, more happiness and more intelligence are the rewards of our journey. Once we realise that, motivation comes. I know.

Level 4	Heart - head (integrated)
Level 3	Emotional management (balance)
Level 2	Mental (involves meaning)
Level 1	IQ (information only)

Fig. 10. The scale of Intelligence

The new age spirituality movement eventually got so tired of the dalliance in the typical new age guru's behaviour that they coined the phrase "walk your talk." Unless we see your insights reflected in your behaviour, we won't listen.

This is good. For quantum spirituality, this "walk your talk" is a must along with the obvious rejoinder, "Don't become a guru unless you do walk your talk."

My friend, spiritual teacher Konstantin Pavlidis, jokingly extends the creative practice of do-be-do-be-do in the very easy-to-memorise chant:

Don't just do-be-do-be-do

Be a walkie-talkie too.

One more thing. However many forays to the supramental you take, the mental-vital representation of it that you make (your soul) and live will always be context bound and so your "transformation," learned behaviour based on these mental-vital representations or brain circuits will never meet with the demands of every situation. In other words, there will always be occasions in which your behaviour will not be appropriate, giving away the fact that your transformation is not yet perfected. For perfection, you need to live intuitively, tangled hierarchically. This is the demand of the next step of evolution of the intuitive mind - the soul level.

Remember that very likely you have been into soul - making for quite a few lifetimes. Why not identify with your character, with what you learn and transfer from one lifetime to another in the form of nonlocal memory rather than with local memory?

Loosening the Structure of the Ego: Humility

"A happy person is not necessarily a human being that is always surrounded by pleasant circumstances, but rather a human being that has an attitude mainly beneficent and optimistic towards life," said Hugh Downs.

We have mentioned ego's structure before: ego, our I/me, is ego/ character/ persona. Character is learned propensities and persona consists of the masks we wear to act with the outside world, the head honcho of our programmed software.

When we completely identify with our conditioned ego at any level of outer accomplishment, we tend to swell up; we begin to think we are "better" than others. We are taking our so-cultivated "I," the head honcho of our simple hierarchy, too seriously. How to break up this simple hierarchy of this accomplished "I?" To undermine the swelled up "I" we bring humour to the game, we learn to laugh at ourselves, we play around our ideas and make fun. This is why Einstein said, "Creativity is intelligence having fun." Fun breaks down the simple hierarchy of the ego/character/persona.

Learning self-deprecating humour also helps us deal with failures which it is said correctly are the "pillars of success." This is why Gregory Bateson said, *humour is halfway towards creativity.*

Humour, especially self-deprecating humour, is also halfway to Wholeness in our archetypal journeys of inner creativity. This is why in the Chinese and Japanese cultures, you see laughing Buddhas everywhere.

The human being is the only species on Earth that has the capacity to laugh. We all know that humour and laughing release stress. When we laugh with all our heart, our negative emotions and contracted states are gone temporarily and this has even the power to heal from various diseases or disequilibria. People often forget how to laugh or even to smile; but truly, humour is an expression of their happiness and inner freedom, helping people to discover the happiness and freedom of life itself. Laughing has also the advantage of being contagious and it comes naturally when people simply are themselves.

To re-emphasise, one of the bigger problems that happens in the spiritual journey of Wholeness is that as we go through the various levels of integrating our acts, even in inner creativity, we tend to develop a sense of accomplishment. The good part of this is that it gives us self-respect and a strong ego to travel further. Unfortunately, with accomplishment, our ego tends to swell up once again. Not good. To bring back humility, I always remind myself, "You still have the habit of picking your nose when you are by yourself. Don't take yourself so seriously." Something like that will work for you too.

No doubt there are difficult moments in life. Homily comes together with the spirit of sacrifice. Comparing us with the others and with what they have will permanently generate the hunger for having more. There are so many who have much less than we do. A wise man said: "I cried for boots, until I saw a man without legs."

As your identity shifts in this way, you will notice that you are kind to others who have not yet made such a shift and are more accepting of their fallibilities. A tolerant quantum spiritual practitioner is a mature quantum practitioner.

Loosening the Structure of the Ego: Developing Authenticity

Expressing Authenticity means that your personas are in synch with your character. In this way, your dominant personas are always expressing your character. As your character changes, so do your dominant personas over time. Allow this to happen, this is important. It enables your ego to engage in creative play with the quantum self in the very important flow experience, which is part and parcel of the creative process, especially at the manifestation stage.

Personally, what I find most challenging about this is adhering to the truth when I tell my personal story when I teach. I know it is important to share my story to add credibility to what I am saying. I have to watch out against the tendency to always fibbing just a little to make my story a little more interesting. Truth may be stranger than fiction, but more interesting it is not, at least not necessarily. Nevertheless, I, and you too, am better off adhering to the truth lest the quantum self is put off by our dilly-dally!

Synchronicity: Expect the Unexpected

The novelist Gertrude Stein once said something to the effect that what changes from age to age is not who we are but what we meet on the road, the chance contingencies. Synchronicity is the name Carl Jung gave to meaningful chance contingencies or coincidences due to a common cause what he tentatively called the "world soul." In the quantum worldview that common cause of events of synchronicity is Unity Consciousness.

Creativity involves in its manifestation stage the movement of flow between the universal quantum self and the creative's personal ego. The movement of nonlocal consciousness in the quantum self that manifests in a creative act can involve more than one person, and events can conspire to give the appearance of blind chance - this is synchronicity.

In the eighties, when I was struggling with transformation and creativity, a new age guru John Lilly said to me: expect the unexpected. My advice to you is the same: Give up predictability and control when you see meaning in a coincidence and respond to the synchronicity. It will show you the way.

Feelings in the Body: the Chakras

We mentioned earlier that when we experience emotion, there is not only a mental thought but also a feeling that accompanies it. What do we feel? We feel the movement of vital energy accompanying the emotion. But where in the body do we feel our emotions? Or, putting it more accurately, where in the body do we feel the feeling component of our emotions?

If you are a connoisseur of feeling you will say, of course that depends on the emotion and also depends on who you are. If one is an intellectual, it is likely that he or she only feels vital energy in the head - brow chakra (fig. 11). When we are being intellectual that is where the vital energy goes.

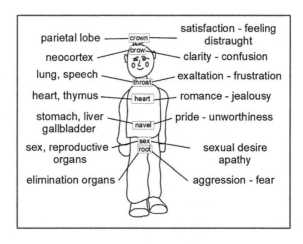

Fig. 11. The chakras

If you are not predominantly an intellectual, then you will recognise other places in the body that you feel your energy. The most familiar of these places is of course, the heart chakra, the place where you feel romantic energy. Can you remember the first time you realised you were in love? Close your eyes and imagine that moment right now; soon you will feel the surge of energy in your heart chakra (felt as a throb, a tingle, warmth, or just expansion). This is the reason why people read romance novels or watch mushy "heart-warming" movies. They (women mostly) like the surge of energy in their heart chakra (which is felt as warmth in these occasions).

In contrast, when men, mostly, watch sex and violence on TV, no doubt their negative emotional brain circuits get involved, but the vital energy goes to the lower chakras as well. If you are sensitive, you would feel it and feel grounded. This could be one reason for the popularity of sex and violence in the media today.

When we feel good about ourselves, we feel an energy boost in our navel chakra; if we feel insecure, we feel energy going out of that chakra - butterflies in the stomach! We feel rooted when the energy moves into the root chakra, but when the energy drains out of there, we feel fear. The sex chakra is where the energy goes when we feel amorous.

After love-making, or after we have a good meal, the energy may rise to the heart chakra; no doubt, women of the old knew this, since they always asked their husband for household needs or money after sex or after food intake. Ever heard the phrase, "the way to a man's heart is through his stomach?"

When we are nervous about giving a speech, our throat seems to dry up; this is because vital energy has moved out of the throat chakra. On the other hand, if you are communicating well, feel the throat chakra. You will enjoy the vibes, we all do.

When we concentrate on something intellectual, our eyebrows focus and you can feel heat in the mid-point of your eyebrows, the location of the brow chakra. Right behind it is the prefrontal cortex where our intellectual thoughts are processed. The feelings are confusion and clarity but they are entirely about the logic of the meaning processing mind.

Our body language can tell us part of the story. When we try to understand something what are we doing? We are trying to remove our confusion. And where do we feel the concentration? You will notice the muscles between your eyebrows are tense. Only when clarity comes, those muscles relax.

In summary, chakras are places in our physical bodies where we feel vital energy localised when we are experiencing a feeling.

The Science of the Chakras

If you examine fig. 11, you will notice that each of the chakras is situated near one or more important organs of our body. This has been noted since millennia. And this is the clue towards a scientific understanding of chakras.

Remember the earlier discussion on V-orgnas? The vital body liturgical fields provide the blueprint for the epigenetic programs of the software that control organ functions. In this way, physical organs perform vital body functions such as, maintenance of the body or reproduction.

Chakras are those places in your physical body where consciousness simultaneously actualises the vital and the physical in the process of which the software programs are run, organ functions take place, the correlated liturgical fields move, and you feel that movement in the form of vital energy.

Here is then a review: A chakra by chakra description of the vital function, the corresponding physical organs and the associated feelings. But do remember, vital energies can actualise only at the navel, at the heart, and at the brow because that is where we have selves. The energies at the other chakras either remain unconscious or are collapsed in conjunction with one of these chakras with a self as these selves awaken in us. Also watch the language: when we say energy goes into a chakra we mean that the energy at that chakra collapses. When we say energy goes out, we mean that chakra is not getting attention, not being collapsed.

The Root chakra: The vital body function is elimination, a crucial component of maintenance of the body called *catabolism*. The organs which express the function are the kidneys, bladder, large intestine, rectum, the anus, and very importantly the adrenal gland. The feelings are feelings of (selfish) rootedness and survival-oriented agression when energy moves in and fear when the energy moves out. Via evolution, the control of this chakra is taken over by the brain amygdala which gives the fear (flight) or courage and aggression (fight) response.

The Sex chakra: The vital body function is reproduction. The reproductive organs- uterus, ovaries, prostate, and testes, etc. and the physical software associated with them are the physical representation of the reproductive function. The feelings are those of sexuality and amour when energy is inward; when energy is outgoing, the feeling is of (unfulfilled) lust. Once again, the control is in the amygdala of the midbrain.

The Navel chakra: The vital body function is maintenance *(anabolism)* and the organ representations are the stomach and small intestine, liver, gall bladder, and pancreas. With upsurge of energy at this chakra, the feeling is pride; when energy moves out, the feelings are anger, unworthiness, resentment, etc. These negative feelings are controlled by the brain's amygdala.

The Heart chakra: The vital body function is self-distinction (the distinction between me and not-me). The principal organ representation is the thymus gland and the immune system whose job is to distinguish "me" from "not me." Here we feel romance when energy moves in. When energy moves out we feel loss, grief, hurt, also jealousy.

Let's elaborate. Why is romance felt at the heart chakra when we meet the appropriate partner? Because now the "me" is extended to include the partner, that's why. There is the thymus gland at this chakra which is part of the immune system and whose function is to distinguish between me and not me. When this distinction is gone because the immune system is suspended, there is romantic love, "You are mine."

Romantic love is still very me-oriented; he/she is important because he/she is mine. This is to be expected. These feelings we are talking about here are the conditioned movement of vital energy, conditioned through millions of years of evolution. When the self- distinction extends to everyone, when everyone is my "family," the heart chakra is said to "open" for everyone and we feel universal, unconditional love that mystics talk about as agape or compassion.

Opening of a chakra signals the activation of new higher biological functions of the organ involved much like how a caterpillar becomes butterfly. The DNA does not change but new genes are activated in order to make new proteins.

The Throat chakra: The vital function is self expression. The organ representations are lung, throat and the speech organs, the hearing organs, the thyroid gland. The associated feelings are: the exultation of freedom (of speech) when energy moves in and frustration when the opposite happens. (You recognise why freedom of speech is considered so important in our culture although real freedom is freedom of choice.)

The Brow chakra: The initial vital function is rational thinking for which the organ is the prefrontal cortex right at the back of the forehead. The associated feelings are clarity of understanding (when energy moves in) and confusion (with depletion of energy).

With further opening, this is the chakra that funnels intuitive energy associated with archetypes that are attracted to you. This is why this chakra is called the third eye or the eye of intuition. The associated feelings of archetypal exploration are satisfaction (when energy is gained) and despair (when energy is depleted).

The Crown chakra: The vital function is body-knowledge for which the physical organ is the parietal lobe.

Of crucial significance is the fact that there is an endocrine gland associated with each of the chakras. The endocrine glands communicate with the brain for the lower chakras. In this way, through this "psycho-neuro-immunological" connection as well as through the autonomic nervous system, the brain gets control over the vital energies at the lower chakras.

In India, there are two ancient approaches to studying the movements of vital energy, Sanskrit, *prana*. The emphasis of the approach of Ayurveda is healing, whereas the emphasis of tantra with which the Ayurvedic ideas of *chakras* and *nadis* (akin to Chinese concept of meridians) became entangled is spiritual awakening. Thus, the writings on *chakras* have become highly confused between these two goals. For example, people carelessly talk about "opening" of chakra through simple techniques of massage. In a way, the language is not wrong. There can be disease at one of the organs of a chakra if the conditioned movement of the correlated prana has become stagnant somehow. Massage certainly can clear up some stagnancy and this can be called an "opening", although it is re-opening really. Or rather just some cleansing. But this is not the opening that tantra talks about.

As mentioned before, there are selves at the navel and heart chakras in addition to the brow. The conditioned movements of prana at these chakras define the vital ego-character we have. This character is hidden by a persona, a very self-oriented one; it's a mask that hides our true self- the quantum self. Tantra is about creatively transforming the conditioned movement of prana and the personalities associated with them altogether.

Practice and Faith

When you start a practice, you believe that the practice will do you good. Then via practice, you develop a new brain circuit of alternative behaviour. How can you be sure you will think of using it right when you are in an emotional turmoil. Of course that is when you need to invoke your newly learned behaviour the most.

This is the same question again: how does a learned behaviour become an element of our character? More and more mastery over the habit we learn gives us more and more confidence, so we can relax and fall into the quantum self. Knowledge that comes from the quantum self has Truth-value which gives us certainty. In this way a mere habit becomes a part of my character.

It can be with building positive emotional brain circuits. Having them is not enough; we have to complement the habit with practice, practice, practice, take the quantum leap, so there is faith. This is hard to do for the kind of character elements we are talking about here; giving or forgiving are not something that you can repeat like you can practice piano. We can take the quantum leap for sure through inner situational creativity - the subject of the next chapter. Then we never fail to invoke a positive emotional brain circuit to offset the effects of an unconscious negative one.

Keys for a Successful Yoga Practice

This is the way I (Valentina) learnt from my yoga teachers, and practiced for over 20 years.

Practically speaking, all our inner states manifest specifically through our bodily attitudes. When somebody is disturbed it shows up in the bodily attitude. In the same way when somebody is happy, that person's body is relaxed and the attitude reflects this state. This observation becomes useful in order to be able to "read" somebody's inner state by his or her bodily attitude.

In time, as a consequence of this fundamental observation, great wise yogis developed a methodology based on assuming bodily attitudes in order to trigger in the inner universe of the practitioner controlled specific processes of correlated inner states. This gives the possibility to be able to have at will and precisely those emotional associations we aspire towards. And it will happen irrespective of our momentary energetic predominance, should we assume the right body attitude.

Considering how the associations are triggered (they are similar to the resonance processes although are actually guided by the nonlocality in the vital-physical bond) and controlled, it comes with no surprise that in the case of bodily attitudes, our inner state can be generated or influenced by the position of the body and by the attention we focus upon this position.

An *asana* (Sanskrit for *posture*) is a position of the body or an attitude that tunes our system in correlation with very precise Macrocosmic energies. In other words, an asana is a "resonating" energetic configuration that we create by arranging the body – and implicitly positioning the energetic structure – in a specific position. In this way, the asana becomes an expression of our aspiration to merge by nonlocal correlation into the energetic ambiance, specifically with the quality of the energies that the asana is in *resonance* with.

When practicing the asana, the bodily posture is firmly maintained, but without tension. The attention is entirely focused to perceive the phenomena of correlation with the specific universal energies. In the same way, with the mind focused upon only one object of perception, the asana maintains the body still and the attention is firmly focused upon only one vital state of association. One of the great advantages from the practice of the asanas from Hatha Yoga derives from this easiness of taming the emotional mind into one position when it is aligned with the position of the body.

Due to a misunderstanding of these fundamental aspects, nowadays many people mistake the asana practice with a mere physical exercise, something practiced in sports class if the teacher has some Eastern inclinations, or in gymnastics with some psychosomatic effects. Yet, there are fundamental differences between asana and physical exercises or even psychosomatic gymnastics. In order to make this aspect even more clear here are some of these differences:

An asana always implies an operating key that will give efficiency to the method. This key consists of the indications regarding the way of focusing the attention during the exercise upon the energetic resonating center (chakra) as well as upon the flow of the energies through the energetic vital body. Sport exercises imply only the attention focus generally on the physical body and particularly on its dynamics, in such a way that the exercise is performed very well.

1. The purpose of a sport exercise is to energise especially our physical structure and, in this way to indirectly induce a state of vital well-being in us. The purpose of an asana is to align our physical structure with our subtle structures, in a sublime aspiration to become aware as much as possible of the supreme state of Divine unity. The inner state that appear while performing the asana is precisely in accordance with the resonances that are facilitated by that asana.

2. Physical exercises do not imply focus of the mind besides the few performance aspects upon which we need to focus in order to perform correctly. After the physical exercise is

repeated several times, one can enter a state of automatic pilot. Even on autopilot, the gymnastic exercise will provide its effects upon the physical body, without much mental focusing required. In the case of an asana, even if we repeat this exercise thousands of times, we need to focus on the vital each time in order to be able to enter in a state of resonance with the energetic macrocosmic center corresponding to that asana.

3. Generally, an asana is a static position, in which the body stays still and relaxed and the attention is firmly focused only on the specific processes of resonance that take place in and beyond the physical body (with rare exceptions, which are special cases). Sport exercises are generally dynamic, with strong movements and with the attention focused only on the physical body in order to ensure a correct performance of the exercise.

To better understand the difference, here is the analogy with the radio. If we take the radio set and we train by lifting it repeatedly to the ceiling and back to the floor, this is what it means to practice sport. If we place the radio in the best position in the room for receiving the signal of the radio station we want to listen to, and then we put on the radio and we pay attention to what the device transmits through resonance, we can say, analogically speaking, that we practice asana.

Considering the above, for an asana to have the expected effect here are some fundamental conditions:

The body attitude must be as relaxed as possible. As known in yoga, the more relaxed is the body the more it allows the energies to flow through and to be harmoniously distributed in the entire structure. Besides, the phenomena of resonance takes place according to its rhythm and all we can do is to become aware about it and in this way to maintain it for a longer period of time. This secret is reflected in the famous treatise *Yoga Sutras* of the great sage Patanjali through the following explanation: "Asanas are mastered through the disappearance of the physical effort and through the fusion with the Infinite."

While performing the bodily posture, the attention is firmly and effortlessly focused on the ineffable processes of complex resonance which is achieved between the practitioner's being and the vital Universe. More precisely, the connection allows new facets of the potentialities of universal vital energies to manifest within the being of the practitioner, making his/her being growing from individuality towards universality. This cosmic integrating awareness makes it so that a state of ecstatic euphoria (the joy of the creative aha moment) is established in the entire being of the practitioner, which cannot be associated to any superficial bodily cause. To illustrate this condition, here is a quotation from the famous spiritually yogi master Vyasa: "Asana becomes perfect through the intimate communion between the practitioner's being and the Universe. Then, the effort to realise it disappears and the couple of opposites is balanced, generating an ecstatic state."

During the practice of an asana, a state of self-transfiguration transforms the vital being of the practitioner. Due to this state of exemplary self-transfiguration the entire being of the yogi becomes a manifestation of the universal "archetype" represented by that asana, a manifestation which constantly tends towards the perfection within itself. The emotional mind and the body of the yogi tend to align in order to make a unitary nonlocal whole with the energies represented by that asana.

After performing an asana, it is important to continue focusing on the specific process of "resonance" for 1 – 2 minutes (this is the minimum recommended, and not necessarily the optimum). In this way, the new attitude induced by the bodily posture – asana – is assimilated and will become available outside of the asana performance, in daily life in how we sit, how we stand, how we walk. Gradually with regular practice, the new attitudes and states become an integrated part of our inner nature.

Yogis say that when these conditions are fulfilled, Consciousness transcends the world of senses and becomes free, spontaneously able to express itself fully, beyond the limitations imposed by the physical-vital and in this way revealing the true ultimate nature of the yogi. This is the real purpose of an asana.

I (Valentina) noticed that performing asanas in this spirit makes the practice effortless, and the posture can be maintained for long periods of time and the benefits increase proportionately, especially on the overall status of health and harmony. The identifying communion which takes place helps us to maintain the asana without getting tired.

Chapter 7

Soul-Making

The practices of the last chapter are all effective to building positive emotional brain circuits good enough to help balance our negativity in general situations of emotion management. We will still get upset and have the flight/fight response to some extent but at least the aftereffect - staying upset - will be reduced.

There is the flight-fight response due to unconscious instinctual memory in the amygdala that then precipitates motor action. The motor action is good if the flight/fight response is appropriate, when there is a real physical threat. Unfortunately, with mind getting into the game with evolution from animals to humans, there are many situations in which the F-responses are just inappropriate. In order to stop the brain from the motor action, we need to make the triggering of the positive emotional circuit automatic; in other words, make it into a learned habit, a part of our character. Situational creativity is a sure fire way of accomplishing this. Soul-making begins here.

Learning how to deal with general situations is not good enough to deal with negative emotional conflicts in intimate relationships. There you need to be specific; there it is more like problem solving except to reach the solution you have to use creativity - situational creativity.

Although formally, creativity begins with the stage of preparation according to creativity researchers, three "I" words play a huge role even before that: Inspiration, Intention, and Intuition. Inspiration is what we experience when with (or even without) reason the quantum self touches us and we feel expanded - a beginning of curiosity. And we make an Intention for such visits more often. It is then that we become aware of our intuitive facility and the law of attraction: the archetypes are attracted to us. And now the work begins in the form of the four stages of creativity. As "I" words they are: Imagination (aka preparation), Incubation, Insight, and Implementation (aka manifestation).

Focused Imagination and Preparation: Preparation firstly consists of catching up on existing knowledge and extending it through imagination. We read voraciously: the good books, current materials on the archetype, whatever we can get our hands on and imagine, imagine, imagine. The idea is to generate new and divergent thinking, ideas that will act as fodder for the second stage of incubation which is unconscious processing.

In the same vein, we listen to lectures by people of transformation, we go to workshops, we talk to like-minded people. Always to generate new grist for the unconscious mill of our mind.

We watch our mental preoccupations; if it is preoccupied with old stuff, we need to clean up our unconscious. Am I putting on a new persona to feel good about myself? Obviously, that will not do. So we clean up our persona, eliminate inauthenticity as far as we can in our present state.

We meditate. There is a meditation that helps us to focus, concentrate on a problem- concentration meditation, meditation on a mantra such as Om for example.

Many people believe that meditation is a complicated technique to be done for hours on end, but this needn't be the case. If you're new to meditation, start off easy – ten to fifteen minutes a day of a simple technique is enough in the beginning. Here is a sample:

Sit comfortably, wearing comfortable clothing. Close your eyes and relax your body. You can start off by paying attention to your jaw; like almost everyone, you are likely to hold tension in this area, so place your attention on relaxing this area. Relax your belly, the shoulders, the muscles around your eyes and allow your shoulders to drop. Take a deep breath or two. Tense muscles all over your body and relax them. Now, place your attention on the following mantra; you can coordinate the mantra with your breathing: Om (pronounced AUM, with silence at the end) as you breath in, and Om as you breath out. Focus on staying present. If you find that thoughts have distracted you, firmly bring your attention back to your mantra as soon as you become aware.

This meditation is called "concentration-meditation" for obvious reasons; it is focusing on an object. You can use not only mantra for your object of concentration but also your breath alone, or a candle flame. Use a small candle and meditate on the candle flame until it burns out.

The difference between a normal "flat" state and a very vivid and alive state is the intensity and length of our concentration upon that state. If we want to have a very intense state of happiness all we have to do is to evoke a state of happiness from memory and focus continuously upon it for enough time; the state that appears will be more or less intense in proportion with the time of our uninterrupted concentration. Concentration-meditation can teach us things like that.

I (Valentina) learnt the fact that the mind needs discipline while the heart needs freedom in order to explore the new. Usually, we are in the opposite situation: our mind runs freely around without control, but our heart is locked away, closed to any contact with new reality. To change this status, we have to train the mind and bring it under control by means of practice of concentration and to learn to let the heart express freely without the mind interfering. The best way to strengthen the heart is via the exploration of LOVE.

It is said in the spiritual traditions that meditation appears spontaneously in the mirror of a mind that reflects a heart full of LOVE. The practice of concentration is relatively easy to build into a success when we love what we are doing. If the exercises are done in a flat and boring way, without "putting heart" into them, the success will not come easy. In this way, the daily practice of mental concentration is a very important help. Even if you only practice a little in one day, the constant practice is a very important aspect of the mental training, firstly because the nature of the mind is to change, and this constancy in practice is helping to regain control over the mind.

A Simple Progressive Technique of Mental Concentration for Learning to Meditate

This is a simple exercise that I (Valentina) often recommend for practice. It is very easy to approach, especially when your intent is clear.

Sit in a comfortable position (in a yoga pose or on a chair), keeping the back and shoulders straight, with the head up so the spinal column is vertical. Choose a simple object that will become the "support" for your mental concentration. Place the object in front of you so that you can observe it easily. Close your eyes and prepare to follow these steps:

- Relax rapidly and profoundly, gradually.
- Observe your respiration and deepen the relaxation until the breath becomes calm and quiet.

- Focus your attention inwards, withdrawing the senses from any exterior stimuli that might distract you. Start by isolating the mind from any thought that may appear. Observe "from outside" any thought that might appear and observe how the thought observed long enough dissolves into the mental background.

- Focus the mind upon the chosen object.

- Empty your mind from all thoughts, then bring the chosen object into the field of attention, without allowing the mind to jump to another object or thought. If this happens, bring it back with calmness and patience.

- Maintain the attention on the object chosen for concentration. Do not force it. Be calm, quiet and focused. Bring the mind back to the object of the concentration when it loses its focus.

- Focus attentively on the object of concentration: approach it with amazement and the curiosity of a child, as if you did not know a thing about it. This approach should not be rational or intellectual, but rather you should get to the essence through feeling and intuition.

- Explore the object in a state of creative silence, without any goal, only waiting for impressions. Then only you and the object will exist.

- Allow yourself to be now in a state of continuous euphoric expectation, accompanied with a high degree of perception. Your being is absorbed in and by the object. Do not try to define, to form opinions or to understand, only be permeable to that object, looking at it as if it were for the first time. This will open you towards the object itself and will create the state of mental receptivity in which intuition (or the superconscious) is able to function. By following this process, you will soon notice that surrounding objects have many meanings and messages that you usually miss. Everything becomes pure wonder, a fascinating mystery that you will gradually unravel completely. You will discover that everything is sustained by an invisible energy and that you can get to feel and control this in time.

When I (Amit) first started to practice meditation, I was like a bird on exploration around a ship in open ocean; fly and fly forgetting about my anchor, my mantra. Gradually this changed. More and more, the mind would remember and return to the mantra. The experience was not linear, not always improving. Some days my meditation would be good and I would feel happy; other days I would have difficulty focusing on my mantra and I would be frustrated. It wouldn't seem like I was meditating at all.

The following Zen story describes the lesson of it all.

A student went to his meditation teacher and said, "My meditation is horrible! I feel so distracted, or my legs ache, or I'm constantly falling asleep. It's just horrible!"

"It will pass," the teacher said matter-of-factly.

A week later, the student came back to his teacher. "My meditation is wonderful! I feel so aware, so peaceful, so alive! It's just wonderful!'

"It will pass," the teacher replied matter-of-factly.

And indeed, although my day-to-day experience would differ as described above, with time I found that there was more space between my thoughts, my mind was slowing down.

We have already mentioned imagination and divergent thinking. In this aspect of preparation, you imagine many possible answers to your problem of finding new meaning of your archetype via extrapolations from your reading and engaging with other people's existing work and even putting some of these ideas in exploratory practices. You can use imagination perhaps for thinking even some semi-original possible answers and put them into practice. You can go to a guru to suggest ideas and practices; many people do. You can use practices suggested in good books: Patanjali's *yamas* and *niyamas*, the *shilas* of Buddhism, the practices suggested in *A Course in Miracles*. You can use Jesus' ideas like *love you neighbor; if he wants a shirt, give him two.* You can only go so far with this "scientific method" *of try it and see.* Life is short, and each practice keeps you occupied for quite long. All this divergent thinking in your conscious life and practices based on them is little compared to what the unconscious can do for you. Divergent thinking is important only because it provides fodder for unconscious processing.

Unconscious Processing

Your thoughts, as soon as you are not thinking them, become waves of possibility. Each thought of divergent thinking is a seed for an expanding quantum possibility wave of meaning in the unconscious. These possibility waves expand becoming bigger and bigger pools of possibilities (fig. 12).

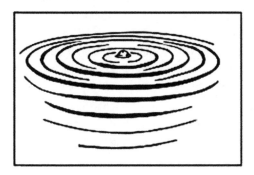

Fig. 12. Quantum possibility waves expand, becoming bigger and bigger pools of possibilities for consciousness to choose from

Waves mix and mingle; possibilities interact with possibilities producing new possibilities. In this way unconscious processing in no time produces a huge pool of possibilities, many of new meaning for consciousness to choose from. The probability of success in finding the right answer obviously is much bigger in this two-stage quantum thinking than it would be with simply one stage conscious Newtonian thinking.

Mindfulness Practices of Being

Unconscious processing can be practiced! If we meditate on just awareness, or be mindful of what is happening in our mind's sky, we relax; we fall into being. I (Valentina) find very useful, simple and efficient for everyone the following practices.

1. One Minute Breathing with Holding the Breath (*kumbhaka* in Sanskrit)

This exercise can be done anywhere at any time, standing up or sitting down. All you have to do is focus on your breath for just one minute. Start by breathing in and out slowly, holding your breath for a count of six once you've inhaled. Then breathe out slowly, letting the breath flow effortlessly out back into the atmosphere.

Naturally your mind will try and wander amidst the valleys of its thoughts, but simply notice these thoughts, let them be for what they are and return to watching your breath. Literally watch your breath with your senses as it enters your body and fills you with life, and then watch it work its way up and out of your body as the energy dissipates into the universe.

If you're someone who thought they'd never be able to meditate, guess what? You're half way there already! If you enjoyed one minute of this mind-calming exercise, why not try two?

2. Mindful Observation

This exercise is simple but incredibly powerful. It is designed to connect us with the beauty of the natural environment, which is easily missed when we're rushing around.

Pick a natural object within your immediate environment and focus on watching it for a minute or two. This could be a flower or an insect, the clouds or the moon.

Don't do anything except notice the thing you are looking at. But really notice it. Look at it as if you are seeing it for the first time.

Visually explore every aspect of this glorious object of the natural world. Allow yourself to be consumed by its presence and possibilities. Allow your spirit to connect with its role and purpose in the world. Allow yourself just to notice and 'be'.

3. Fully Experiencing a Regular Routine

The intention of this exercise is to cultivate contentedness in the moment, rather than finding yourself caught up in that familiar feeling of wanting something to end so that you can get on to doing something else. It might even make you enjoy some of those boring daily chores too!

Take a regular routine that you find yourself "just doing" without really noticing your actions. For example, when cleaning your house, pay attention to every detail of the activity.

Rather than a routine job or chore, create an entirely new experience by noticing every aspect of your actions. Feel and become the motion of sweeping the floor, notice the muscles you use when scrubbing the dishes, observe the formation of dirt on the windows and see if you can create a more efficient way of removing it.

Don't labor through thinking about the finish line, be aware of every step and enjoy your progress. Take the activity beyond a routine by merging with it physically and mentally.

The Key is Do-Be-Do-Be-Do

Do-be-do-be-do is alternative doing and being, preparation and incubation. Why alternate between doing and being? Being brings relaxation; conscious processing stops, the unconscious picks up the slack. Too much relaxing takes the focus of your unconscious processing away from your problem. Like an evening fire in the fireplace on a winter day, the fire needs occasional stoking to keep it going. "Being" has to be interrupted by more doing occasionally to bring the focus back.

It helps to simulate do-be-do-be-do via alternative concentration-meditation and mindfulness meditation both introduced above.

Sudden insight: Quantum Leap

When consciousness chooses a new answer, you get a surprise making it clear the choice is discontinuous; you have taken a quantum leap. In situational creativity, you are working within the archetypal context already established by earlier researchers, the paradigm you are using.

Archetypes come with truth value; when we directly encounter them as in the experience of insight in fundamental creativity, there will be certainty. In situational creativity - looking at new meaning in a given archetypal context, you get a surprise, a new meaning, and conviction that the choice is right. Unfortunately, as a situational creative, you are a little hyperactive, do-do- do. It is in your pattern to be impatient and force your unconscious to make an actualization even though the required gestalt of possibilities to solve the problem is not there yet. In this way, in all likelihood, the choice that comes to you especially in the beginning can be erroneous; what you thought was an 'aha' surprise and conviction was simulated by ignorant exuberance.

In outer creativity what people do is to use the scientific method at this stage: try it and see. And most scientists work within an already existing paradigm, and indeed they use the scientific method - experimental tests -routinely, and this is one reason why they have been so unreceptive to acknowledge the importance of unconscious processing or the importance of quantum in creativity.

Placebos, Doctors, Gurus and Psychotherapists

What does an inner situational creative do to check out if a new meaning arrived at via the creative process is the right one to put in serious practice and make a brain circuit and embody it? Try a behaviour change and see? Not very practical, is it? It will take a long time to try every new idea of change that comes to you as "fake" quantum leaps. The new thought really did not surprise you, but you rationalised. This is why spiritual traditions emphasise a *guru*; they say a *guru* will tell you if your insight of new meaning is the right one for you.

How does the guru tell you? The guru can tell you because you are following the guru's particular take on the archetype. In the wisdom traditions, gurus are supposed to be people who are transformed, who live by intuition, and so they can also tell you by that keen power of intuition.

Where do you find such gurus in today's world? (Rarely, some people do). Well, you can use your own intuition; that is one choice. Better use a transpersonal psychotherapist or a guru's guidance for the whole process. There is a reason. It is called *placebo*.

Placebo is much misunderstood. It is said to be healing produced by sugar pills via mental belief (faith would be a more appropriate word here) because your doctor gave you the sugar pills but you didn't know; you believed you got "real" medicine; you have faith in a doctor. It is quite effective for temporary relief in chronic diseases.

Is it just mental belief that gave you faith? No. The truth is, a chronic disease is created by wrongness that you create through errors in your life style that give rise to vital and mental software not good for the physical body organs. And you in your higher consciousness have the ability to heal yourself. The same erroneous lifestyle also robs you of your confidence in your healing power. So you depend on a doctor to heal you.

When a doctor gives you sugar pills without telling and you think you are getting a medicine, your belief in the doctor and the medicine (a faith, really!) restores your healing power. The rest is situational creativity, although you may not be consciously participating in it.

If you go a transpersonal psychotherapist you trust, it can work the same way as the placebo effect. This is how the guru system used to work in India, Japan, and other places (the shamanic cultures) so well in the past. The gurus were skilled psychotherapists and transpersonal to be sure. They had expanded consciousness that includes.

Are there such transpersonal psychotherapists today? A few perhaps, but not many. We need to train them in large numbers. This is one of our main functions at the transformative educational universities we are founding.

To summarise the creative process for situational creativity for inner work:

1. Preparation, divergent thinking about an archetype as contextualised by a wise teacher (guru) or tradition or a psychotherapist of transformational training.

2. Unconscious processing using divergent thinking of new meaning of your given archetypal context as seeds that sprout.

3. Do-be-do-be-do.

4. Sudden insight with 'aha' surprise and conviction.

5. Working with a guru or a psychotherapist for guidance. You may have misjudged your *'aha'*. Try out insights that the guru or psychotherapist recommends and see if it works. Likely, you will require more than one try.

6. If an insight works to change behaviour in the appropriate direction, great. If it does not, back to the drawing board.

Creativity in action: How you Develop Positive Emotional Brain Circuits

Emotions are feelings plus meaning – thoughts - that mind ascribes to the feelings. Emotions also produce physiological effects such as facial expressions that arise in a particular emotive state. We cannot control our feelings or physiology so easily, so mystics through the ages have mostly talked about controlling the thoughts associated with the feelings. This is called *developing* a virtue in the spiritual traditions. Along with meditation, developing virtues is the job of traditional spiritual practice.

Let's talk about developing loving kindness, or what we simply call Goodness. For example, you are experiencing the feeling of anger in response to provocations of a certain bully. You have angry thoughts, "I will show him," and all that! Mystics say, cool it. Cool your anger by replacing the indignation with love.

Jesus said, "Love your enemy." Upon seeing your enemy, anger and violent feelings arise along with associated thoughts of hate; the result of the negative emotional brain circuits. If instead of thinking hate, you think love, the negative feelings will also subside, mystics say.

Try it! If you can do it, it may surprise you by changing the energy of the interaction. Pay attention, thinking love energises your heart chakra. This is an example of psychoneuroimmunology - mental thought affecting the immune system and suspending it, arousing the feeling of love in the heart chakra.

Alas! There are problems with this approach. First, it is not easy to think loving thoughts when an enemy is confronting you. Helpless flight-fight or freezing is part of instinctual behaviour. You are helplessly constrained to think hate. Second, even if you have a little control by strengthening the brain area involved, your anterior cingulate cortex (ACC) via meditative practices, before you act you would like to have a guarantee that your loving thought is reciprocated by the enemy. If the enemy remains violent in spite of your nonviolence, does that not make the situation worse because the enemy interprets your behaviour as weakness?

Mystics remind us that we should give up such bargaining and try to practice "unconditional" love (taking into consideration boundaries of course, especially in the beginning). Then how do you practice unconditional love? We have to do it step by step using the creative process of situational creativity.

Jesus knew it too. His first counsel is, "Love your neighbour." How do you love your neighbour? Jesus explains. If he wants a shirt, give him, two shirts. If he wants you to walk with him a mile, walk two miles. Like that. Do it paying special attention to your heart chakra. Feel the energies there, as you do your practice; don't be mechanical. Do this with as many other variations as you can think of. Each act of such unconditional compassion produces memory, memory in the body and memory in the brain. These memories are what I call *positive emotional brain circuits.*

How do you produce other variations of the practice in the same spirit as Jesus' suggestions? This is where the creative process comes handy. First engage in some divergent thinking: variations you can imagine, like asking the person to dinner, etc. And then wait. Your thinking will act like pebbles in a pond and each will create many possibilities of practice for your unconscious to choose from. Do-be-do-be-do. The unconscious can choose a gestalt; it can also choose a combination, a superposition of possibilities. And then choice and insight, a new practice.

This is how situational creativity works. This is essentially how loving, kindness, meditation works too. Prolonged mindfulness meditation increases the gap between thoughts; in those gaps there is unconscious processing. The meditation practice becomes like do-be-do-be-do. Then insight and implementation.

Every such new practice creatively invented by you will make your positive emotional brain circuit stronger.

What happens when you have positive emotional brain circuits to balance the negative? When your negative emotions arise, with your ability of mindfulness, you meditate, not express, not suppress. Just stay aware. That brief time, the gap you are now allowed between the rising of angry emotion and motor action, will enable the positive emotional brain circuit to come to your rescue. You recover quickly. Then you can use reason.

This is exactly what positive psychologists have discovered. We never can rid of negative emotions. Story is that even Ramana Maharshi, a great sage in India, used to get emotionally upset with some of his disciples. Having positive emotional brain circuits help you to recover quickly.

This is transformation, the beginning of soul-making. You have been initiated in emotional intelligence. You are at level 3 in the happiness spectrum.

I (Amit) used to have a temper. If upset, I'd stay upset for a long period. It was a major struggle in my early relationship encounters with my wife after we got married back in the seventies. At her coaxing and at the demands of my transformational journey, as I began to build positive emotional brain circuits following more or less the steps above (although I did not know much about the creative process then) under my wife's guidance, I noticed how emotional intelligence works; I still lost temper, but my mood swings did not last long, usually no longer than some minutes. This is what emotional intelligence is about, an intelligence that makes it easier to maintain intimate relationships.

On the same note, I (Valentina) sometimes used to remain upset for long periods of time as well and I was also very impatient. I, too, have experienced a prolonged struggle in my efforts to transform myself and this behaviour and eventually received first-hand learning of all that later on has made me able to help others through their growth, happiness and health trials. We can indeed transform the dominance of negative brain circuits into a dominance of the positive, once we choose to live, for example, in gratitude, following our discovered meanings and archetypes. Synchronicities, love, forgiveness, gratefulness and compassion come along and make of life a truly divine game.

Chapter 8

The Professional's Path: Karma Yoga Quantum Style

The quantum activist professional looks for a way of finding congruence between thinking, living, and how to make a living via her profession, assuming that the profession is a match with her dharma. This of course is the essence of quantum activism if the professional uses quantum principles for making the changes necessary.

According to the Bhagavad Gita, the recipe is Karma yoga- the yoga of applying the idea of spiritual transformation right smack in the middle of real life. *Karma* means *action* and *yoga* means *integration* in this context. Karma yoga is designed to integrate your actions with the rest of your life - thinking and living, exactly what a quantum activist is attempting to do. The strategies of the two are perceived by many traditionalists to be quite different. Why?

Maybe the traditionalists misunderstand the Bhagavad Gita. To them, the goal of all spiritual practice is self-realisation, realising you are no-self. They make Karma Yoga into a yoga of selfless service. Karma yoga interpreted in this way is an important practice of many spiritual traditions even outside Hinduism, especially of Christianity, and Soto Zen. Why? Because the goal of all these traditions is 1) self-realisation - to shift your ego identity from the ego to the quantum self and 2) God- realisation - living in unity. Karma Yoga need not be such a thing. A fighter needs a strong ego, not no-ego. The idea of karma yoga, quantum style or Bhagavad Gita style, is not to "kill" the ego, but to use the ego in creative service in play with the quantum self.

The protagonist of the Bhagavad Gita, Arjuna, is engaged in a war in which he has to fight warriors who might even be greater than him. The only way he can prevail over them is via creative action, action that follows from akarma - inaction. What is inaction but doing nothing, while being so that unconscious processing can take place leading to creativity.

You don't engage in your profession for satisfying your ego-persona either; you don't ask, "What is in it for me?" before you act. The strategy is to undermine the ego persona's simple hierarchical control.

For a quantum activist, your actions are meant to transform both you and the world, serving yourself and the society with evolution in mind. Rabbi Hillel put it well:

If I am not for myself, who am I?

If I am only for myself, what am I?

In conventional spirituality, the wisdom is that we can only change (transform) ourselves, not the world. The world is unimportant anyway. We try to change ourselves through selfless service to undermine and eventually kill the ego. In quantum activism, the goal of self-transformation is to become empowered to change the world also. Because we have created the world, we can recreate it. If recreation is in synchrony with the evolution of consciousness, our job should be relatively effortless.

For the quantum activist, the ego needs to be strong, having an extensive repertoire of learned contexts, in order to participate in the creative journey of recreating the world. Of course, we have to bring ego to authenticity, so that the ego can act in synchrony with the quantum self. This means giving up those aspects of our persona that are not consistent with our character. Of course, we still also work on negative traits of our character and on reducing ego's control over unconscious processing, how else can God find an opportunity to encounter us and help us change?

One of the famous instructions of karma yoga as enunciated in the Bhagavad Gita goes like this: *You* have only the right to act, not the right to the fruit of the action. The traditional interpretation according to many is to surrender the fruit of the action to God. Traditions make a big case for desire-less action *(NisKama karma)* as if that is possible short of self-realisation and manifestation thereof. The fruit of the action is accomplishment, it does not have to be material accomplishment, however; accomplishments of the subtle - more courage, more conviction, more command over your skills, more learned repertoire, more loving charisma - makes the ego strong - a "can do" ego. This is good for creativity. This is good for leadership. The meaning of the verse is different for the quantum activist: If you fail to get any fruit of the action, don't be disappointed. WHO will get the fruit, benefit from your creative act, is up to the purposive evolutionary movement of consciousness. This way of interpreting the words of the verse inspires us to engage karma yoga in professional work, right in the middle of our workplace, just like Arjuna did. We don't compete as the materialist does. Instead, we cooperate, because we don't worry about who gets the fruit of the action.

The workplace may not be conducive to your karma yoga, you say! Well, what is your activism for if not for bringing change to wherever it is needed?

It is a fact that all our social institutions in which most people work today have lost their way from idealism to materialism. Aren't most workplaces by necessity places dedicated to earn a profit and make material gain? you say. Yes, but what is the material gain for? Is it not also for the well-being of the workers and people of our society? The problem is that driven by materialist beliefs we have limited the definition of our wellbeing to our own survival needs and even that within the context of the material domain only. If well-being is extended to include our higher needs following Maslow's idea of hierarchy of needs, the subtle, our institutions easily can become places for karma yoga - quantum style.

Doing your karma yoga practice this quantum way at work has a great advantage in that it enables you to integrate the outer and the inner. You use inner creativity in the exploration of your archetype to change yourself via your practices in living; you use outer creativity in the exploration of the same archetype in your profession.

In the industrial/technological age, the necessity of mass production has made the job of ordinary people repetitive and monotonous. Practicing karma yoga while working on the assembly line is easy to talk about, but not easy to carry out. In advanced economies such as the United States, Europe, and Japan, and even in developing economies like the BRICS countries, we are just about ready to get out of the industrial/technological age to a advanced technological age when machines or robots will relieve us from routine mass production assembly line jobs. That and other factors such as ecological awareness are increasing the scope for creativity on the job like never before. With this kind of development the future for doing karma yoga in the workplace seems bright.

Your particular context for quantum activism then depends on how you choose to make your living. For example, if you are a businessperson, clearly business is your arena for quantum activism. It is suited for you only if your dharma archetype is abundance.

You have to choose your livelihood carefully. Ask, is this way of making a living a suitable vehicle for my creativity, my nonlocal needs of social consciousness, and my commitments to intimate relationship through which I work on transforming my simple hierarchies? And most importantly, does this way of earning my livelihood bring me meaning, create avenues for me to explore and express my dharma, and give me satisfaction?

The co-founders of the New Dimensions Radio, Michael and Justine Toms put it this way: "In the Thai language there is a word, *sanuk*, which means that whatever you do, you should enjoy it." Processing old meaning is robotic information processing, mechanical, at best joy-neutral, usually boring. How do you find joy except by replacing information processing by meaning processing? When you process new meaning, when your intuitive facility is engaged, then; because then, the brow chakra vital energies (of clarity and satisfaction) are also engaged. When you process new meaning that you love, then additionally you engage the heart chakra, your consciousness becomes expansive, and you experience bliss or spiritual joy.

The next question we ask is this: Is the practice of our profession serving the purpose of evolution? If not, we attempt to change the ways of our profession. Theoretically by understanding where the field of our profession went wrong and how to right the wrongness. Experientially, by putting our understanding in practice by activist efforts. And this we do always in conjunction with our personal transformation on the job in mind. We try to leave egotism out of our activism, for example.

When we stop measuring our accomplishment in material terms and learn to enjoy our subtle character accomplishments, we count our subtle abundance as much as we value material abundance; we no longer have to be a numero uno, we no longer have to have more abundance than others, or seek power to dominate others; only then can we seek meaning without violating our values; only then can we engage in action to fulfil our dharma.

To deal with our accomplishment orientation the quantum way, the key is not to give up the ego, but not to take the ego too seriously. In one of the issues of the comic strip Mutts, one of the canine characters say to another while looking at some birds flying, "How do birds fly?" "Because," the other canine responds, "They take themselves lightly."

Balancing the Qualities Called Gunas

In a previous chapter, we introduced three ways in which we can process meaning: *sattva, rajas,* and *tamas.* Sattva is to process meaning engaging fundamental creativity - creativity consisting of the discovery of new meaning in a new archetypal context. *Rajas* is to process meaning by engaging situational creativity in which we look to invent a new meaning but only within known archetypal contexts. Finally, we can also process meaning within what we know, within our conditioned memory, without seeking new meaning. This is *tamas*, the propensity to act according to conditioning. All these qualities of mind are referred to as *gunas* in Sanskrit.

Talking about people of predominant rajas. There was this joke about the degrees that our universities, mostly driven by the energy of rajas, bestow upon us: B. S. - you can guess what it means. It takes four years of accumulation of the stuff to get the B. S. degree. Another two years of more of the same to get an M. S. Finally, spend another five years at accumulating it; now the stuff is piled high and deep, so you get a Ph.D.

People of rajas in no time will make things very complicated; so complicated that people of tamas fall behind. Look at the difference between college educated and non college educated people today and you see the difference between rajas and tamas.

Traditionally, likely due to the influence of weather and climate, Western people are dominated by rajas and the Eastern people by tamas. However, a modicum of people in the East are people of sattva (which they use mostly for spiritual exploration). However, a modicum of people in the West also are people of sattva but the rajas dominance of the culture restrains them to outer creativity - outer accomplishments,

Nowdays, due to modern technology weather and climate need not have such influence on our mental habits. Yet, partly through the sheer force of inertia of socio-cultural conditioning and partly due to the materialist malaise that continues to dominate us, Westerners have not responded in bulk to this technological advance. However, as a quantum activist, it would behoove you to begin the practice of balancing your three gunas - sattva, rajas, and tamas - as soon as possible. It would behoove you to provide leadership in this area.

For Westerners, what this boils down to is to learn to relax, giving up the do-do-do lifestyle and make do- be-do-be-do your living mantra. Only then fundamental creativity opens up to you, the door to love and goodness opens wide, and the beacon of conscious evolution becomes clearly visible. However, giving up on outer accomplishments is against the grain of the Western culture; this is why materialism has taken root here so fast. The two reasons that the society can even entertain the idea of inner change now is first, because the zero sum game is over, the limits of material growth have caught up with us, and second, because the paradigm shift in science from primacy of matter to the primacy of consciousness is upon us. Nevertheless, we quantum activists have to lead the rest of the culture in this respect; we have to change the social systems so not only material outer accomplishments are valued but also subtle inner accomplishments are valued.

An important aspect of developing sattva is diet. As you know the body proteins are our promoters of action. In this way a protein rich diet promotes rajas, the empire building quality and the pursuit of power with the objective of dominating others. No wonder, several years back, a protein rich diet touched a popular nerve in America where most people covet rajas and actively cultivate it towards the pursuit of power and abundance for their own numero uno. For a quantum activist who is interested in fundamental creativity including spiritual transformation, a diet with only moderate protein intake is better. In other words, not only keep away from saturated fat (which grows tamas), but also keep away from excessive protein and develop a diet rich in complex carbohydrates, fruits, and vegetables. Moderate protein intake, by making room for sattva, allows you to channel your power to positive use such as empowering not only yourself but also other people to engage in meaning processing.

Quantum Activism in The Arena of Your Livelihood

The Bhagavad Gita begins with what sounds like a simple recipe: acting without the guarantee of the fruit of the action. Towards the end of the book, when we get the entire teaching Krishna says that to accomplish that simple goal of developing equanimity about the fruit of the action one has to cultivate *sattva* and also balance all the gunas- *sattva, rajas,* and *tamas.* In other words, one has to combine simple *rajas*-dominated activism with fundamental creativity and *do-be-do-be-do* exploration of the archetypes without any one's guidance. This is quantum activism at its highest fruition.

In traditional societies, people who make their living in service jobs mostly engage the quality of conditioned tamas, their conditioned repertoire is all they need and all they are encouraged to use. This is the job mentality that elitist societies promote for predominantly tamas dominated people they want to keep that way. In these societies, people who earn their living in business and trade, are mostly driven by the conditioned instinctual emotion of greed for increasing their material possessions (in other words, love of money). They are also partly driven by rajas, the tendency to expand their "empire."

Business people are dominated by tamas mixed with a modicum of rajas. They serve the archetype of Abundance but they use situational creativity only to make money and building conglomerates. People of politics are people predominantly driven by the quality of rajas in search of power and they use power to build their personal empires and dominate others. Their rajas is tainted by tamas in the form of the negative emotion to dominate, and egotism to serve their own numero uno. People of predominant sattva engage in the professions of teaching - worldly knowledge and spiritual- the profession of healing (excluding cosmetic healing), and of course, in professions requiring fundamental creativity explicitly - arts, science, music and dance, justice, and mathematics.

This socio-cultural fixity of match between a person's guna and the profession he or she engages is very resistant to change. As quantum activism becomes more prevalent in our societies, people will balance their gunas more and more, and they will engage in all these professions with all three gunas. Only in this way, shall we be able to come out of the guna stereotypes of these livelihoods. Only then winds of change can engulf the arenas of our livelihood, our workplaces, and evolution towards large- scale exploration and embodiment of the archetypes can proceed en masse.

Chapter 9

Integrating the Three Fundamental Dichotomies: The Path of the Quantum Leader

What keeps us most from decision-making which is a major leadership quality? What makes the decisions good for the follower, ultimately good of everyone? One major reason is that we all suffer from various dichotomies of which three fundamental dichotomies stand out. These are: 1) the transcendent-immanent dichotomy; 2) the inner-outer dichotomy and 3) the male-female dichotomy.

The transcendent-immanent or above-below dichotomy is the dichotomy between creativity and conditioning. In the Bhagavad Gita, Krishna says to Arjuna, action (conditioned actions) that follow from other actions (conditioned also) are non-actions. They don't count. Only actions that follow from non-action, from the transcendent unconscious, in other words creative actions, count. Of course, the conditioning also does count, in the sense that it gives us a repertoire of skills or expertise to draw from to prepare and manifest our creative ideas. In this way we need to balance creativity and conditioning. The Chinese call this *balancing yin* (transcendent or creativity) and yang (immanent or conditioning).

This dichotomy is much exacerbated in the people of the twenty-first century: the emphasis on information and the denigration of meaning and purpose; the do-do-do conditioning dominated lifestyle, the banishment of passion and enthusiasm—vital energy and intuition, from our lives. We need to replace do-do-do with a do-be-do-be-do lifestyle.

Creativity is the way quantum leaders get their conviction: they know. Creative insights come with certain knowledge; there is truth-value in them.

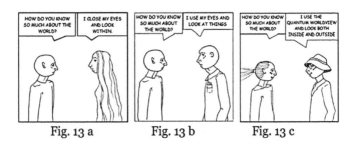

Fig. 13 a   Fig. 13 b   Fig. 13 c

The inner-outer dichotomy is also huge in today's people no thanks to scientific materialism. Long time ago, in a book named *Precision Nirvana,* I saw a cartoon whose spirit I have tried to capture in fig. 13 (a) and (b). This illustrates the polarising view of traditional spirituality: the outer is for materialist; the spiritual seeker must close their eyes, a process that Patanjali called *pratyahara*. Like a tortoise, you bring your outward tendencies inward. Then only spirituality.

We differ. The spirituality of a quantum leader calls for the integration of the inner and the outer (fig. 13 (c). How do we do that? There are many ways: below I will discuss three of these ways.

The male-female dichotomy is first of all a problem of 1) navel-heart dichotomy. Among their body selves, males use the navel chakra more; women work with the heart self. 2) head-heart dichotomy. Male prefer thinking; women, feeling.

Balancing Inner and Outer: Right Relationship with the Environment: Shallow and Deep Ecology

Hopi Indians are famous for their emphasis on right relationship, not only with people and things but also the environment at large including that of the whole planet.

In the inward journey of conventional spirituality, right relationship with the environment is much ignored. No doubt this has led to the modern movement of ecology - our ethical responsibility must extend to the whole biota of the earth, Gaia.

The root Greek word for "eco" is "oikos" meaning the "place we live" and "logy" comes from Greek logos meaning "purposeful knowledge". Ordinary ecology is about the knowledge of our physical environment. We live not only in a physical world, we also live in the three subtle worlds - vital, mental, and supramental. Deep ecology in this way refers to the knowledge of both our external and internal worlds and it asks us to have ethical responsibility for all of these environments that we live. It is also about integrating inner and outer.

Deep ecology is meaningless if you hold to scientific materialism because in that worldview there is no internal experience that is meaningful or relevant. Only matter- external reality matters.

Only when we become established in an evolutionarily ethical relationship with all our fellow human beings, it is time to ponder our ethical responsibility to all creatures, great and small, including the responsibility to our non- living environment. Only then it makes sense to ask, What is our responsibility to the planet earth, to Gaia?

Deep ecology requires not only abiding by a few rules for preserving our ecosystem or passing a few governmental laws preventing environmental pollution, but also taking actions to change our internal environment that enables us to engage in shallow ecology. Lack of good internal hygiene - for example, prevalence of me-centeredness and negative emotion of greed, is why people do not see the importance of shallow ecology.

Deep ecology practice is wonderful preparation for creative transformation, creative discovery of Wholeness. When you take such a quantum leap you realise one astounding thing: I choose, therefore I am, and my world is. The world is not separate from you.

When we do this en masse, we will leap into a truly Gaia consciousness which has already arisen in human vision from a different context (I am referring to the Gaia theory of the chemist James Lovelock formulated in 1982).

Balancing Inner and Outer: Mental Hygiene

The yoga psychologist Uma Krishnamurthy emphasises mental hygiene when she says, "Emotions are more contagious than bacteria and viruses." So we must avoid contamination of negative emotion, and by the same token, of negative thought as part of good hygiene for the subtle bodies.

The concept of mental hygiene is an important part of deep ecology and it is something that I (Valentina) first heard about from Swami Advaitananda; this concept completes the moral or ethical basis of deep ecology's principles. Just like the body's state of health and harmony is based, among other things, on a preventive attitude that implies maintaining a good physical hygiene, in the same way an adequate psycho-mental health, which makes any training easier, is based on maintaining a hygiene on the psycho-mental level of a person. It can be easily noticed that, although maintaining hygiene at the physical level has become a well-known fact of society, maintaining a state of hygiene and purity at the psycho-mental level has not yet found its place in humanity. This is due especially to ignoring the consequences of a chaotic psycho-mental activity upon the harmony and health of the human being, as well as to the almost complete absence of educational methods that allow the purification of these levels and the maintenance of a state of purity.

The fundamental principle of the purification processes is this: "the speed of removing the impurities must be greater than the speed of their accumulation (or pollution). At the mental level, this is done simultaneously from two directions: by constant purification and through behaviour that reduces the process of mental pollution. Firstly, by daily practicing mental concentration exercises."

The key is the ability of paying attention. Whenever we don't pay attention, consciousness collapses our thoughts from our memory bank on the average basis, probabilistically, as dictated by quantum science. Parasite thoughts and preoccupations then appear in the field of our awareness; we follow them unconsciously. These are gradually removed when we learn to pay attention to our inner sky. Secondly, we aim to remove thoughts that appear against our desired movement of consciousness: useless discussions, images that do not help us in any way or that put us in state of occult resonance with aspects we do not want in our being, and which are impurities of the mental/emotional structure. Thirdly, on the positive side, we attend, satsang, the company of people of transformation, to give us inspiration.

Balancing Dream and Waking Life: Dream Psychology

What is a dream? A dream is part of an ongoing life that we live in the meaning dimension. Dreams are investigations, explorations of meaning. In the waking life, there is too much information in the physical that takes away too much of our attention. The ongoing storyline that we build for our life because the physical has this Newtonian habit of fixity also has the effect that we don't pay much attention to the meanings that we are exploring, the propensities that we are developing for our explorations. The melodramatics over the storyline takes too much of the time.

Dreams give us a hint of what meanings we are exploring, what propensities we are developing, that kind of thing. Part of becoming enlightened through living in the quantum way, call it quantum living, is to pay attention to dream states. As we do that, in addition to acquiring the sensitivity to the transition between changes of states of consciousness, we find more and more that we have what is called *lucid* dreams. There, we can indeed use the dream states for developing solutions to problems of the waking state. This is sign of inner-outer integration.

During a dream, we have experiences of different characters — people and things. Dream objects; they all stand for something — the meaning you ascribe to them in your life. For example, you might see in the dream your wife or girlfriend. But that would not be your actual wife or girlfriend visiting you in their astral bodies. What is visiting you is the meaning you ascribe to the wife or girlfriend. All these meanings are appearing in the dream in the guise of dream characters. In the dream, of course, we don't experience them at the meaning level. We experience them in the same way we experience them in the physical waking life. That habit is still there. We experience a dream episode as if it is being enacted in physical reality. When we wake up though, we can look at the dream from this meaning point of view. That was not really my girlfriend, so what was it, what meaning do I give to that particular girlfriend? I give this meaning. She represents, symbolizes, this meaning to me. For instance, she could be a bit of a shrew. This shrew part of me is the meaning she represents in my dream.

Another character in the dream may be representing the miser in me, the part that refuses to be generous. Another character may be something completely different such as courage, me being brave. In this way, we analyse the meaning of the dream symbols and what they are doing, then we discover something; a pattern begins to emerge, giving me insight about where I am in the quest for the meaning of my life.

In 1998, I (Amit) was researching a "New Quantum Science of Dreams" through a grant from the Infinity Foundation and Institute of Noetic Science. What did that entail? I did this research with the psychologist Laurie Simpkinson. We established a dream group at IONS; that also helped. A paper we wrote together was never published, but I included the gist of the paper in my book *God is not Dead*. Briefly, we were able to show via a lot of case histories that dreams are indeed ongoing reports of our meaning life. We also arrived at a new classification of dreams: physical body dreams consisting of what are called *day-residue* dreams of stuff for which we do not arrive at closure during the day; vital body dreams connected with suppressed emotional trauma; mental body dreams, ongoing reports of our meaning life; supramental dreams involving images of the collective unconscious giving us hints about our archetypes; and spiritual dreams hinting at our oneness with everything.

I will give some examples from my own dreams. When I was beginning to change from a materialist to someone who integrates the material and the spiritual, for a while, I dreamed an ongoing series of purgation dreams. This went on for months. I was always dreaming of lavatories, men's rooms, toilets, and the idea of course was that cleaning up my system of toxicity was very important in my process at the time. My system had a lot of materialist waste in it, so my dreams were creating attention for cleaning it up. Like what the Jungian psychologists call shadow cleansing. Or what we earlier called *mental hygiene*. I was not getting it, initially. When it became clear after a lot of dream analysis that, yes, my system needs to be cleaned up, and I became dedicated to cleaning it up, the purgation dreams stopped.

In the last dream that I had in this series, two characters appeared. One was Ronald Reagan, the archetype of conservatism, and the other was the actress Jane Fonda of ultra liberal vintage. But what stood out in the dream, is not who the characters were. Well here is a president, and here is a famous actress, all they were doing was dancing around detritus. Literally. The ground they were walking on was full of excrement. I woke up with the feeling that okay, being liberal or being conservative is all shit. It is following somebody else's opinion. And I was ready to give up somebody else's opinion influencing who I was. My slate was thus clean, so I could get into discovering my own opinion about stuff, integrating liberalism and conservatism, through real creativity-fundamental creativity. After this episode ended, I never saw another excrement dream.

For others, in a different context, the dream of toilets can also mean letting go...not suppressing. It all depends on where you are stuck at the time.

Previously, I discussed male-female dichotomy. Carl Jung theorised that this dichotomy is rooted in humankind's collective unconscious in the form of anima archetype of female in men and the animus archetypes of males in women. Jung advocated that males integrate their archetype of anima in themselves and females cultivate the archetype of animus.

As a male, at a certain period of my life, I was feeling emotionally all dried up, very intellectual and very brain centered. And then one night I had this dream. I was looking for water, searching, searching, and then I found this stream but as I got closer, I found that the stream was all dried up. I was very disappointed, and then a voice said, "Look behind." When I did, I was surprised; it was raining. I ran into the water enjoying it falling all over my body and then I discovered a young woman had joined me, a delightful pretty woman. We walked together for a while thoroughly enjoying the rain and each other's company. Then we arrived at what appeared to be the place she lived and she said goodbye. Seeing the disappointment in my face, she added, "I am going to London for a while. I will be back."

When I woke up, I immediately recognised the young woman as the representation of my *anima* and felt excited about finding emotional fluidity once again in my life. Of course, it did not come immediately. "She went to London." But she did come back in my life soon after.

Finally, I will give you my one example of an unmistakable supramental or spiritual or "bliss body" dream that happened to me in the nineteen eighties. In this dream, I was feeling very joyful, and then I saw the source: a radiant man radiating joy that I could not get enough of. And that was it; that was the dream. When I woke up, I consulted my dream teacher, and he looked at me kind of funny with big eyes, and said, "Amit, don't you understand? You were dreaming of your own enlightened self." That was his interpretation. After all this time, I think I was dreaming of my supramental body called *sambhogakaya* body in Buddhism.

How I Discovered the Selves in My Body

Do we have Self-identity at the chakras? We said in chapter 1 that we do. It took a long time to truly realise that.

Recall again that your experiencing self is tied up with the engagement of a tangled hierarchy. And that requires a cognition and memory apparatus such as in the neo-cortex. Initially I thought our visceral experience of the feeling has to wait until mind gives meaning to the feeling and tangled hierarchical quantum measurement takes place in the neocortex; only then you experience feeling, always mixed with thought, as an emotion. This is how most people experience feeling as we have discussed in chapter 1.

But wait! While men generally accept that their self is centered in the head, quite a few women claim that their heart "talks" to them because they know how to listen to their heart. Is this mere metaphor for these women's emotionality or is there a scientific basis for it?

The plot thickens further when many mystical traditions refer to the spiritual journey as a journey towards the heart. Many spiritual traditions insist - Christianity, Hinduism, Tantric Buddhism, and most Shamanic traditions- to name a few major ones - that all great spiritual masters have an awakened "heart." A recent example is Ramana Maharshi in India who insisted that the self is located in the heart.

An important question for quantum science as I was developing it became this: is there a self of the heart? In view of the fact that most humans are so tied up with the self-identity firmly located at the neocortex does the heart talk-positing a self of the heart-make sense? And here we must heed what the women half of the world's population says. Many women would agree with the mystic and would say, Yes Charlie, there is a heart!

I am now convinced there is more than a metaphor here. There is a self of the heart. Here is a quick synopsis of how we all can reach that conclusion.

First, the immune system is the second most important body organ. Scientists are discovering that the immune system has quite a bit of autonomy.

Second, everyone knows the neocortex needs sleep every night; sleep depravation is bad for both physical and mental health. It is easy to connect the thymus gland (of the immune system) with romantic love; romance is when the immune system function of distinguishing between me and not me is suspended. Why do we need love? The answer must be this: to give the immune system some needed rest. If the immune system is denied rest, immune system malfunction will occur and this leads to many disorders such as autoimmune disease, heart disease, and cancer.

Notice that the neocortex and the immune system need regular rest. What do they have in common? The neo-cortex has autonomy; it also has a tangled hierarchy and thereby it acquires a self. The immune system has autonomy; does it also have a self, does it have a tangled hierarchy?

A big surprise of neuroscience is the recent discovery of a big bunch of neurons at the heart chakra that the HeartMath Institute has been attracting our attention for some time. There is a cognition system at the heart chakra - the thymus gland; the feeling of love is an excellent way to cognise. With the bundle of nerve available, there is also the capacity to make memory. Cognition and memory are the two systems that make a tangled hierarchy in the neocortex; and the heart has them too. So, the heart chakra does have a self: consciousness can and does actualise experience - pure feeling of love - in the heart chakra by itself. Without the brain's help.

One day, Valentina called me with the news, neuroscientists have also discovered another little brain, another big bundle of nerves at the navel chakra. The human gut is lined with more than 100 million nerve cells - it's practically a brain unto itself! Navel chakra has a cognition apparatus, it cognises the feeling of pride or self-worth. Its little brain gives it a memory apparatus. The combination makes a tangled hierarchy and manifests a self-identity centered at the navel.

The Japanese culture calls the navel center *hara*, the self of the body; at least one spiritual culture has recognised even this center of the self for hundreds of years. To be fair, even in our modern culture, creative men do talk about gut feelings that tell them about the veracity of an experience.

Does the navel chakra have autonomy? Yes, some. Does the navel chakra need rest? Yes, of course. Periodic fasting is a must; we should not eat continuously.

The important question is why do we (at least the male among us) not hear the small voice of the heart and women the small voice of the navel chakra, these pure feelings associated with the actualisation of experience at these chakras? I think this has to do with evolution and culture and is perhaps the main contributing factor for the male-female dichotomy.

The Explanation of the Male-Female Dichotomy

Finally, we are ready to explain the male-female dichotomy. It is a fact that the two sexes process things differently. "Men are from Mars, women are from Venus," one author joked, but it is not only a joke.

Sometimes, we refer to this male-female dichotomy as head-heart dichotomy. Men are centered in the head while women listen to their heart. Could this be purely cultural? Under the aegis of scientific materialism and overuse of information technology, millennial women in America get offended if they are labeled emotional. Obviously, the culture is changing. However, I still think there is more than culture here, too.

When we were hunters and gatherers, men got the big food items, they certainly were physically more imposing (still are), so they dominated (there is that domination circuit built into the brain). Men were security and survival provider for which the navel chakra is essential. Women, on the other hand, had to nurture children, had to hear the dictate of their heart chakra. In this way, there is a biological component to the male-female difference, and it became a part of our collective unconscious.

Mind you, and this is the sad part, women do, quite naturally, have access to the self of the brain as they must; but when we went from the vital era to the mental era, powerful men (the male aristocracy and the religious oligarchy) forbade women from meaning processing, and this sad story continues even today although the women's liberation movement in the nineteen sixties did help the women to balance the head and the heart a little.

In this way there is also a cultural contribution to the male-female navel-heart and heart-head dichotomies. Traditional societies encourage little girls to give love to others to prepare them for eventual maternity to be sure, but it prevents women to develop identity with the navel self. In contrast boys are pampered; they are encouraged to be narcissistic. Therefore, men have some awareness of the navel self (many men report gut feeling in creative experiences), but not much awareness of the self of the heart.

The creativity researcher Mihayil Chikszentmihayili writes, "When tests of masculinity/femininity are given to young people, over and over one finds that creative and talented girls are more dominant and tough than other girls, and creative boys are more sensitive and less aggressive than their male peers."

I (Amit) declare, both sexes have both a 'head' which expresses as the voice of reason, and 'heart ' which gives us the voice of positive emotion coming from the body. I think, the reason both men and women in our culture are so ignorant of a feeling-self (men more than women), is that by itself the navel or the heart, cannot compete with the self of the brain, whose dominant voice drowns out the tiny voice of the weak of the body. So there is lot to be integrated here to get a proper balance of the male-female dichotomy.

When women feel both with their heart (other love) and with the navel (self-love), they are balancing the two chakras. When men are engaging in other love, they are balancing their navel with their heart.

So far, so good. However, after such balancing, the navel-heart combo in the body is still about feeling, about love. And here biology again biases the female towards a relative dominance of the body navel-heart self compared to men. This has effect on how they think.

It is a fact that men think objectively whereas women's thinking is relationship oriented, an influence of the body self no doubt. For men the body self does not seem to influence the brain self.

Carl Jung theorised that the dichotomy of the sexes has its origin in the collective unconscious. When our ancestors were connected enough (as our illustrious ancestors of the vital mind era of human evolution were) to make the collective memory that Jung calls the *collective unconscious*, they universalised the human sex difference.

As Jung has correctly theorised, the male potentialities (of both thinking and feeling) appear in the female as the archetype of animus; similarly, the female potentialities (of both feeling and thinking) appear in the male as the archetype of *anima*. Jung advocated that males integrate their archetype of *anima* in themselves and females cultivate the archetype of *animus*.

Not only does this makes sense, it jives with an anima dream I had in which anima showed up as a young woman in my dream (see above). Apparently, many men see *anima* dreams and it is a young woman that fits the image of a suppressed self perfectly. Same for *animus* in women.

We can then conclude that *Male-Female* or *Anima-Animus* integration is a two-step process: 1) integrate and harmonise the navel and the heart; 2) integrate and harmonise the body (loosely call it *the heart*) self and the brain self.

Why is All this Important: The Path of Quantum Leadership

A leader has to lead all people contrary to the very partisan practice of the current crop of political or business leaders we encounter. Yes, a business leader explores the archetype of a Abundance. If the business leader does not integrate his life style to include feelings and intuition, his exploration will be way tilted to material abundance alone contrary to the need of quantum economics and the quantum society.

In the same way, a political leader explores the archetype of power. Unless she integrates seeking power with seeking love, she will use the power for herself and domination of others contrary to what democracy and quantum politics demands. Only the exploration of goodness and love can give her the necessary mindset to use power to empower others as the institution of democracy requires from our leaders.

A leader has to serve both male and female of the population. Moreover, there is the question of how to behave with the opposite sex when you are in a position of power. Sexual misbehaviour is rampant today among political leaders. This can be corrected only if leaders stop the use of sexual charisma to communicate and replace sexuality with love. It also helps if leaders go ahead and integrate the male and the female, the navel and the heart self. How to do it? See later.

We need quantum leaders who are aware of these dichotomies of the human condition and are dedicated to do something about integrating them. Only then the leaders can lead their people to avoid the perils of these dichotomies on a mass scale.

Chapter 10

The Healing Path: Quantum Healing and Exploring Wholeness

Quantum worldview says we have not one but five bodies: physical, vital, mental, supramental (soul), and spiritual (made of *ananda*, the expanded consciousness of the quantum self and unity consciousness). Therefore, disease from the quantum point of view is at least in part due to a lack of synchrony between the different bodies. Healing would then consist of restoring the synchrony. In other words, any disease is a lack of Wholeness of the five bodies acting as a whole; and any healing is restoring the Wholeness.

Vital body medicine in the form of Reiki, yoga, herbal medicine, acupuncture, and homeopathy, provides us with examples of restoration of wholeness via situational creativity in the vital arena, involving vital energy movements. In the past we have misunderstood it much. For example, when Walter Cannon talked about "wisdom of the body," he must have really meant the placebo effect we introduced earlier - our own healing power. Andrew Weil, likewise, writes about body's healing system, an "innate potential for maintaining health and overcoming illness." Maintaining health is a characteristic of our conditioned systems, body-energy body-mind trio, we can think of this as our placebo power also.

In simple terms, what happens in this kind of healing is this: the Reiki healer's energy, the vital energy of the herbs, the energy of the homeopathic medicine, the somewhat random vital movements in the case of acupuncture, all become potentialities to mix and mingle with the existing potentialities generating many new ones in our unconscious for consciousness to choose from. Our healing intention or placebo power is enough to activate the unconscious healing choice.

In mind-body disease, wrong mental meaning produces a vital body energy block, producing dysfunction of the physical organ correlated with it. We cannot heal the wrongness of the mind by staying at the level of the mind. This is where we have to employ fundamental creativity-discovery of a new representation of the archetype of Wholeness-to provide a new archetypal context of mental meaning. This involves exploring the archetype in suchness, not with somebody else's representation of it.

There is ample evidence of spontaneous healing with little or no medical intervention. They are example of spontaneous creative quantum leaps of healing. The wrong meaning spontaneously gives way to clarity of a creative insight to heal the vital energy block and the immune system is restored with such force that even an overnight ridding of a malignant tumour can take place.

The physician Deepak Chopra calls this kind of healing "the result of a *quantum leap*" and hence *quantum healing*. Chopra is right; and if it is a quantum leap, indeed a protracted creative process should produce the same result as suggested in *The*

Quantum Doctor. This idea has found verification in many reported cases. You will soon find more details on this subject in our upcoming book, Goswami and Onisor, *How to be your own quantum doctor.*

We have also suggested in the above-mentioned books that such quantum healing can be used as a healing path to spirituality by not only the patient but also the physician involved. The patient's case is obvious provided the patient is willing to make lifestyle changes consisting of integrating the various conflicts of life that produced his or her disease in the first place. That integration obviously acts as preparation for further exploration of the archetype of wholeness. How about the doctor?

Most healers come to their profession with a deeper intention than doing a job although this is somewhat hard to conclude assessing allopathic medical practice today with doctors bogged down via rules and regulations and fear of malpractice. Healers, most allopathic doctors included, want to heal themselves to a higher level of Wholeness that they currently live; they too are exploring the archetype of Wholeness.

In this way, if the patient and the doctor explore the archetype of Wholeness together such as a research project between a professor and a graduate student at a university, if they are correlated, they both will feed new seeds of potentialities to their common nonlocal unconscious. The seeds will expand via unconscious processing becoming new pools of possibility for consciousness to choose from. And a quantum leap of fundamental creativity can happen.

The entrance requirement for the nonlocal unconscious of previously uncollapsed potentialities is achieving quantum correlation between doctor and patient. This requires a major change of the current trend of a simple hierarchical medical care where the doctor dictates everything. This simple hierarchy has to give way to tangle hierarchy.

Therefore, for the healer, for the doctor, the purpose of the creative venture of healing is to discover tangled hierarchy of relationship with people, no less. This is why we call this "the healing path to spiritual transformation."

Patients: See Disease as Opportunity

Indeed, the healing path to spirituality is the traditional path for the creative exploration of the archetype of Wholeness. When you heal from a disease via situational or fundamental creativity - physical or mental - you are exploring the archetype of Wholeness.

No kidding. Many mind-body healers think that disease is a creation of the patient. "What have you gained by creating your disease?" is one of their favorite questions to a patient. This, I think, is going too far because this kind of question only confuses the patients and makes them feel guilty aggravating the separateness that disease represents.

The mind-body healer has a method in her accusing her patient in this way: she is seeing an opportunity here that the patient needs to see if he or she is ready for it. More sensitively put, the question is, "Now that you have the disease anyway, instead of giving it a negative spin, can you give a positive meaning to it? Suppose you take the responsibility for the disease right or wrong and ask, why did I create this disease for myself ? what do I want to learn from it?"

The Chinese ideogram for the word crisis stands for both danger and opportunity. In disease, perhaps you only see danger - the danger of suffering or even death.

Can you make this instead into an opportunity to probe deeper, probe into your conflicts and incongruences that you need to integrate. That would begin your journey of exploration into the supramental domain of consciousness in the form of the archetype of Wholeness.

A disease is an expression of enormous incongruence. In a physical injury the software of the injured organ becomes incongruent with its vital blueprint and this affects negatively the feeling of vitality of that organ. Your feeling of illness is the expression of this incongruence. If the disease is a creation of wrong mentalization of feelings, the incongruence will pervade all levels-mental, vital, and the physical. It is like we feel something, we think something, else, and we act in still another way.

A news reporter was working on an article on Gandhi for which he attended several of Gandhi's lectures. So impressed was he that Gandhi did not consult any notes while delivering his lectures, he asked Mrs. Gandhi about that. Mrs. Gandhi said, "Well, us, ordinary folks, think one thing, say another, and do a third - but for Gandhiji they are all the same." What she was trying to say is that Gandhi was congruent as to thought, speech, and action. He had explored the archetype of Wholeness to fruition.

How do we reestablish congruence so that the mind, the vital energies, and the physical representations act in congruence? The answer in a nutshell is: explore the archetype of Wholeness to completion - do-be-do-be-do, insight, and implementation.

It is true. A mind-body disease is a very loud wake up call, to awaken to the exploration of Wholeness. To be sure it is like being hit by a two-by-four, but it is supremely effective. Yet, so far very few people have successfully used it.

I (Amit) knew one such person, I have spoken of him in *The Quantum Doctor*. Swami Vishnuprakashananda of Rishikesh was a renunciate searching for God realisation when he fell so ill in the gastrointestinal system that he could not eat anything for twenty-nine days. An intuition told him to go and lie down at the Anant Padmanava temple in the South Indian city of Trivandram, and he did. Suddenly, a vision came to him, a quantum leap to the supramental took place in him and he was healed. After this, his context of living changed forever.

For a while, my wife and I used to take spiritually interested Westerners to visit spiritual centers of India under the auspices of IONS travel department. Swamiji, who was still alive, always did a reenactment of his experience for the sake of our visitors and danced around saying "all bliss" and all of us did the same thing following his enthusiasm. Bliss always descended, so great was the energy of his transformation.

Read my book *The Quantum Doctor* where there are discussed many cases of quantum healing, both spontaneous or effected by using the creative process, for further insight how Wholeness comes about in a quantum leap in all cases of quantum healing. If the healed now engaged in the manifestation stage of creativity beginning with a lifestyle change, much spiritual transformation would result.

When we engage in the exploration of Wholeness in acts of creativity, we can use a quantum leap of creative insight to the service of outer creativity, or we can use to explore ourselves, in inner creativity. We can only be interested in healing our disease; that would be engaging in outer creativity. But why limit the application? It is entirely possible to use the search for Wholeness in the creativity of the mental/vital/physical domain with the objective of spiritual growth. Then it is like inner creativity, it is great. Read the physician Bernie Siegel's book, *Peace, Love and Healing*, for many anecdotes about inner creatives who followed this path from disease to healing to wholeness.

For many of us it is not necessary to be sick before we heed the call of Wholeness. We can start with health and creatively explore the mental/vital/physical. Or just the vital/physical. There is an entire spiritual tradition in India and Tibet that is based on this latter idea. I am talking about *tantra*. The martial arts developed in China and Japan have a similar objective.

Healing as Regaining Wholeness

The essence of the new paradigm of healing is that one must look upon the physical body as the material expression of the spirit. From this perspective, the health problems are only messages sent to us by the Spirit through the physical body in order to become aware of the level we have on the path of evolution.

From this new perspective, I (Valentina) emphasise that the physical body is the mirror which is helping us to see the state in which our spiritual life is. Therefore, any real healing process has to begin with learning the spiritual lesson of the illness we are confronted with and then gradually to eliminating the cause–which created the illness.

In antiquity, the state of health was the one which people were more aware of and now we are more aware about disease. Therefore, in the modern time if we don't have a disease, we invent it. And because of this reason, because of people focusing mainly on the disease and not upon their status of health, the emptiness became full and the full became empty. The disease which is the absence of health became…something while the health became the absence of the disease. And this situation of course is putting the whole system upside down, is turning from an optimistic system into the pessimistic system. Nowadays we see the empty half of the glass instead of seeing the full half of the glass. Any process of healing begins with a deep understanding of this fact.

Interestingly, the word "healing" has the same etymological root as Wholeness. This means that healing in the ultimate sense is achieving Wholeness. What does this imply?

Patanjali said that all our suffering comes from ignorance, ultimately. The ultimate disease, the root disease, is the illusory thinking that we are separate from the whole which is what Patanjali calls *ignorance*. To heal the disease of separateness is to realise that we are the whole, we have never been separate, that the separateness is an illusion.

After one has healed oneself thusly, one can even heal others. The philosopher Ernest Holmes, who founded a healing tradition called *Science of Mind* knew that the healing of another does not take will power, but the knowing of Truth: "Healing is not accomplished through will power but by knowing the Truth. This Truth is that the Spiritual Man is already perfect, no matter what the appearance may be."

However, it would be wrong to say that the realisation of Truth automatically heals a pathological condition of the physical body (of the realised) for which the separation (for example, structure) has enormous inertia. What the realisation does is to free the realised from the illusion of identity with the physical body, from the illusion of identity with any suffering, be it disease or death.

Chapter 11

Wholeness Through Nutrition

In this materialist culture, when we speak of strategies for good health, we include good hygiene, good nutrition, exercise, and regular check up (with a conventional medicine expert of course). We are really speaking of caring for the physical body. It is important no doubt.

We spoke of good mental hygiene. Just as physical hygiene tells us to avoid harmful physical environment, similarly, mental hygiene consists of avoiding pollution of the psyche. The positive side of that is the nutrition of all our subtle bodies - vital, mental, and soul.

Nutrition of the Physical

What about the nutrition of the physical? Here there is clear conflict of interest. Food is one of our pleasures if you are addicted to your gross body and to the philosophy of scientific materialism. And too much physical pleasure in the form of pleasurable food is not good for nutrition.

There is an old Hungarian story. Two old fellows are talking. One guy says, "Oh, this gout; it has hit me again." The other guy snorts, "I have told you before and I will tell you again. Eat nutritious food like I do and you would never suffer from gout." Now it's the other guy's turn to sneer, "But, my friend, you got nutritious food to suffer from everyday."

We, of quantum science, take the view that when you have found your way to subtle happiness, you can strike a middle ground. If you are satisfied with only moderate amount of pleasure from food, it is possible to satisfy both taste and nutrition requirements.

This section will be looking at how to nourish the physical body, how to pay attention to the food we take with both nutrition and pleasure in mind.

From a quantum science perspective, the point isn't that we should be changing our food and body-appearance to meet an external standard, but rather it is to get in touch with ourselves and our authentic needs. Whilst we do make some very basic nutritional recommendations, these are not rules or strict guidelines for you to adhere to. This journey is not about 'you must eat this and not eat that', but is about asking your body and mind what it needs to feel nourished.

Food does serve a two-level function: nutrition and pleasure. We believe that both of these factors need to be met in order to achieve physical nourishment. Our cells need adequate nutrition to function optimally, so fresh, natural foods with good vital energy are recommended.

Certain energetic conditions, giving thanks or saying a prayer before eating also raises vital energy of food. I (Amit) was in India in 2016, teaching a Quantum Activism course at the Pyramid Valley in Bengaluru, where research is being carried out looking at the effects of using pyramid amplified vital energy to preserve tomatoes for longer periods. Whilst out there, I sampled a 140-day old tomato which had been sustained under a pyramid that was designed to feed it amplified vital energy. To my surprise, the tomato tasted relatively fresh. Fresh fruits and vegetables with good vital energy will of course have an impact conducive to optimal physical overall health.

It is also worth noting that vegetarian food has a higher vital energy (moreover it is relatively undifferentiated) than non-vegetarian food and, and fresh unprocessed vegetarian meals digest more easily too. We must remember that when we ingest meats, not only are we ingesting all the chemicals that the animal was given prior to being slaughtered, but we are also ingesting the negative emotions that the animal endured before and during the slaughter-process. I call beef raised the American way *angry beef.*

Aside from addressing the vital energy in food, we must also give consideration to our beliefs and intentions surrounding food. How you feel about the food you eat matters. When in India, I often overeat along with all the international students that join me; we all eat three high-carb, satisfying pleasurable vegetarian meals a day for ten days with snacking in between, and yet no-one on the team gains weight. The reason? I think it is because we are satisfied on every level. The meal itself is fresh and balanced, incorporating all six tastes recommended by Ayurveda: sweet, sour, pungent, astringent, bitter and salty. Well ok, not much bitter. Given that we have an inbuilt mechanism to seek pleasure, this combination of food is perfect at providing the pleasure factor.

By the way, I am not recommending overeating. The most important signature that you have not overeaten is the feeling of expansiveness that should follow every meal that nourishes you. Look for it every time you eat. This is when pleasure gives way to happiness.

Nutrition of the Subtle

Nutrition also must include the vital and the mental. Since fresh food (cooked and uncooked) has more vital energy than stale or even refrigerated food, fresh food is to be preferred. In the same token, a good case can be made for vegetarianism when we consider nutrition at both, the physical and the vital body levels. Especially when you consider the way we manufacture meat and poultry in this country, you have to worry about the vital energy you get from these products. Eating the meat of a fearful and unhappy animal of negative vital energy can only bestow you with negative vital energy: anger, lust, fear, insecurity, competitiveness, etc.

Nutrition of the mental means feeding ourselves good literature, good music, poetry, art, what is normally called *soul food.* They are no less important than regular food. Entertainment that provokes laughter and joy is to be preferred than that which makes you feel "heavy." That is the general rule of mental nutrition.

How do we exercise the vital and the mental? Here the Eastern traditions have contributed much towards the exercises of the vital body. Hatha yoga postures and breathing exercises called *pranayama* have come from India, Tai Chi and chi gong from China, and Aikido from Japan. But, as Uma Krishnamurti emphasises, do not engage in these exercises with hurry in your mind. Relax instead. Slowing down and paying attention to your inner space of vital energy is the objective. Valentina has provided in this book a few series of important beginner recommendations in preparation for such approaches and the Quantum Yoga course that we have developed further ponders on these aspects in an integrative way.

For the mental body, the exercise is concentration- for example, mentally repeating a mantra such as "*om* (AUM)." You can practice it during work, or you can sit and do concentration meditation as in TM practice. Concentration is work and it tires you out until you discover alternating concentration with relaxation- do- be-do-be-do style. In this mode, prolonged concentration is possible without tiring the nervous system out.

And do-be-do-be-do occasionally will get you to the flow experience when we dance with the quantum self, when quantum leaps to the supramental is likely to happen. This is then the exercise for the supramental body.

In my workshops, I often lead participants in a flow meditation by following an idea that originally came from a Christian mystic named Brother Lawrence. Brother Lawrence, who was a simple-minded and good-hearted cook, used the practice that he called "practicing the presence of God" to attain enlightenment. In my version (Amit's), you begin by sitting comfortably. We do quick body awareness exercises to bring the energy down to the body. Now you bring love energy to your heart. You can do it in a variety of ways. Think of a loved one (your primary relationship) or of a revered one (for example Jesus, Buddha, Mohammad, or Ramana Maharshi), or simply of God's love. Once you feel the energy in your heart, diffuse your attention (like you do from focused eyes to "soft" eyes). Let some of your attention go to peripheral activities that are going on around you, sounds, sights, even chores. Let it become a flow between your soft attention at the heart (being) and the stuff of doing at the periphery. Imagine yourself taking a shower with a shower cap on. The water wets you everywhere, but not your hair. Similarly, the worldly chores grab your attention away from feelings at all the chakras, but never from your heart. Once you get a hang of it, you can do what Brother Lawrence did, live your life in flow.

Occasional creative quantum leaps are important also for the mental body, because only then the mind gets to process the truly new meaning because of the new context involved. There is a story about the impressionist artist Rene Magritt. Magritt was walking on a street when a display cake at a confectioner's window sidetracked him. He then went inside and asked for the cake. When the shopkeeper was bringing out the cake in the display case, Magritt objected. "I want another one." When asked "why?" Magritt said, "I don't want the display cake because people have been looking at it." Likewise, it is healthier for your mind not always to process only those thoughts that everyone is processing. Hence the importance of creativity.

For the bliss body, the lazy person's exercise is sleep. When we wake from sleep, although we feel happy, we remain the same even though we enjoyed being without subject-object split. This is because only our habitual patterns of possibilities are available for us to process unconsciously during ordinary sleep. This changes when we learn to sleep with creativity in mind. Then states can be reached which are sleep-like, but when we wake up, we burst with inner creativity, we are transformed. This "creative sleep" is the best exercise for the bliss body.

And if you are serious about positive health, don't forget getting good dosages of inspiration from persons of good positive health—this is called *satsang* in India. For a person interested in positive health, *satsangs* are more important than check-ups or encounters with diagnostic machines in a doctor's office.

Chapter 12

Wholeness Through Integrating the Perspectives of Living and Dying

Every culture has its own Taboo subjects, such as "Death". Here is a comment that I (Valentina) love about this subject from the text of *Mirabilis Mundi:*

"There are some subjects that we are alienated from, as a culture. Alienated in the sense that they are avoided tendentiously. One of them is death. We are mesmerised into believing in eternal youth. So we have built a net of images that are continuously projected on ourselves, which we unconsciously ingurgitate daily: media image is of a youth that is more youthful from decade to decade. We live in a society of uplifting, wrinkle decreasing creams. Even the more or less spiritually orientated choices of life have suffered from this blinding infusion and we are facing the Enlightenment rush (believing that it gives us individual existence as immortal being) or How to avoid death [with] spiritual agendas.

Why are we running away from death? It is the most inevitable thing that will happen to us in our life. The human society used to have rites and tales about death. Today, still unexplained fully from the scientific point of view, this part of life is covered and we are taught to postpone facing it."

What will happen if people's awareness would be turned towards becoming conscious that we are approaching death with every minute we live? Would our life become more meaningful? Would we stop chasing material fortunes, be less individualistic, care more for the loved ones, love more, be present more, here and now? Would we stop running blindly to work and back, and kids, and loans for cars and houses, and stress and high blood pressure, and divorces, and loneliness? Would we be able to stop the circle from moving? Would the awareness of the inevitably approaching death give more meaning to the moments when we truly love, when we truly see, when we touch the face of the ones we love – the child we gave birth to, the mother elder now, the friend, the lover? What would we do differently? How would we build our lives as an individual, as a family, as a community, as a society? What would be our priorities, our values?

The life we live is our power and strength, our force of transformation due to the mystic hiatus called *death*. And here stands the whole magic: we become eternal not by running away from death, or denying its inevitability but by passing through it while still alive.

As certain advanced esoteric yoga trainings and the Tibetan Bardo tradition made me (Valentina) aware of, many people fear Death because in reality they fear Life. Many fear Life because they fear Death. And in this way the only life strategy they have is to survive it. However, this keeps them away from living life and enjoying its amazing lessons. These people have to become aware of the fact that surviving our life is not the same as living our life.

Indeed, what can be more stupid than trying to get away from the most amazing experience that we are given on this planet: our own life. Some pretend they are living their life just because they are doing all kinds of things (albeit some of them are meaningless or sometimes even stupid), or they are doing anything that crosses their mind. This is just another way to survive; it is a survival kit that has anti-boredom and anti-depression (anti-suicide) program based on entertainment attached to it.

As Swami Advaitananda emphasizes, remembering about death is not possible without remembering about life. Life and death are the two faces of our existence. This is why the ancient "memento mori" is at the same time "memento vivere" as an ultimate act of awareness. He who is not aware of Death will also not be aware that he is alive. Even if it seems simple, by attentively looking around you will notice a lot of people who are more like robots, their life being replaced with a lot of schemes that keep the machine running on autopilot. Yet we are constantly reminded about life and death by the problems that we face in our everyday life, when we are not attentive to them and they take us by surprise. When we are awakened and transformed, we become attentive to our life (and to our death), and then the problems of living life or facing death lose their scary appearance and simply become phenomena which we detachedly contemplate and learn lessons from.

Death becomes a taboo not because it is so scary (for there is no reason for this), but because nowadays people have become so attached to life that they don't dare to live it! And not living enough will increase the anxiety of facing Death. The idea "the more you save the more you have" (an idea that seems to be suggested to us by all the real life situations – see the current crisis that is leading many to this conclusion) makes many people unconsciously try to save life for later. It has somehow become the instinct of citizens throughout the world today to live life on 'economic mode' in order to save it for later. Yet, something tells us deep inside that this is not according to the fundamental experiences that make us human beings. For instance, love teaches us another lesson: in love the more you give the more you have!

Everyone has experienced this at least once and could intuitively understand this principle. We can see from this perspective why the first unconsciously accepted principle in life ("the more you save the more you have") is going against Life itself and somehow makes us avoid (save) our life and thus fear Death that in a way becomes inevitable.

How often do we deny reality as it is because it is not according to our expectations, projections, concepts? Then we try to save reality itself for later, putting everything on autopilot and go to sleep in a kind of protective psycho-mental-hibernation until life (with all its disappointments and unpredictability) is gone and we are ready for departure. Instead of being ready for departure we feel that something is wrong and we've missed something: Life! And then again, the phenomenon of Death appears to be a scary, premature, unwanted, unnecessary, brutal end to Life. And we try to hold on to it even though there is no quality to it. If we had lived with full intensity all this time, Death would have shown us a different face.

If there is one cause that drives health care costs in America up and up and up, it would be, according to many people, the money we spend to keep people alive in the last three months of their lives. Death is not only regarded as painful and undesirable, but essentially as an encounter with the great void, nothingness, a finale. And there is the source of the fear of death.

Then there is the issue of survival after death and reincarnation for which there is now huge supportive data. In spite of that, scientific materialists deny life after death and hence prolong the divide between science and religious traditions that believe in life after death.

A science within the primacy of consciousness settles the debate very quickly. Consciousness is the ground of being; it never dies. Additionally, we have the subtle bodies, the mental and the vital of which the individuality arises from conditioning. When we look at the mental and vital conditioning, we find that this is the result of modification of the mathematics, the algorithms that determine the probabilities associated with quantum possibilities. The "quantum" memory of these modifications is not written anywhere local, so it can survive the local existence in one space-time to another, giving us the phenomenon popularly called as *reincarnation*. What survives then are not bodies, but propensities of using the mind and the vital body, propensities that are popularly called *karma*.

Why do we reincarnate? Because it takes time to awaken to supramental intelligence. It requires many permutations and combination of vital and mental patterns (that Easterners call *karma*) and many quantum leaps to eventually learn the contexts that constitute supramental intelligence.

It is this karma, in the vital and mental respectively, that explains why we are born with mental gunas (and vital gunas too although I won't go into that subject).

What is Death in this perspective? Death is an important part of the learning journey that we are in. For one thing, death gives us a new physical body to make new embodiments of the archetypes. Death can also be a prolonged period of unconscious processing.

Chapter 13

Vital Creativity in Search of Wholeness

Let's continue with the subject of vital Body Disease and Quantum healing. Once the vital functions are built in as software into the physical body hardware, the organs, we forget the supramental contexts (the vital functions) and the vital blueprints that are needed to program the organs and keep them smoothly running. When we deal with the conditioned movements of a living organ, we can even afford to forget consciousness, the programmer. When something goes wrong with a program, what then? As an ongoing example, keep in mind the case of the immune system program of killing abnormal cells that cannot stop replicating themselves going awry, causing cancer.

We need to realise three underlying causes for organ dysfunction. The cause could be at the mental level. For example, the mental suppression of feelings at the heart chakra will cause the malfunction of the immune system program and cause cancer. This we have already discussed. The cause could also be at the physical level, a defect of the representation making genetic apparatus of the body. This we will take up later. The third possibility is that the vital blueprints, in our example of, the immune system programs, no longer work, because the contextual environment of the physical body has changed. This we cannot fix by the techniques of conventional vital body medicine because of the contextual leap involved. We have to invoke new vital blueprints for the same vital functions for coping with the new context. But for this we need the guidance of the supramental.

We need to make a quantum leap from the vital directly to the supramental bypassing the mind. The supramental is the reservoir of the laws of vital movement and vital functions. There is a whole probability distribution full of vital blueprints that consciousness can use to make representation of the same vital function. We use the quantum leap of creativity to the supramental to choose a new vital blueprint to take form that fits the new context. This new vital blueprint then enables the creation of new programs to run the physical organ level or even the rebuilding of the organ itself (regeneration) to carry out the required vital function.

Now the crucial question. If quantum healing involves creativity of the vital body, can we develop a program of action for healing ourselves based on this idea? What would the creative process entail in the case of the creativity applied to a diseased vital body that will take it from diseased to healing?

One problem is that few people today have access to their vital body movements, let alone taking quantum leaps in the vital arena. Preparation is needed, perhaps even more rigorous than in mind-body healing.

In analogy of mind-body healing, the purpose of the preparation stage is to develop a purity of intention of healing (a burning question at the vital feeling level), to slow down the vital body that has to heal, and to create an openness and receptivity towards feelings. There are techniques of slowing down vital energy flow - pranayama exercises developed in India and Tai Chi and Chi Gong movements developed in China are examples.

How do we work to open up at the feeling level of our being? Through intimate relationships. Burning questions will follow when we pursue relationships with utter honesty. This may involve allowing your partner to express feelings freely. You may wish to see the old movie, *The Stepford Wives* in which husbands made their wives into conditioned robots so that they would be compliant. The fact is, in the Western Culture, both men and women do this to their mates (women to a lesser extent) in the emotional arena. To do the opposite is a lot of challenge indeed.

At the next stage the patients and their doctors would try various new (new to the patient) techniques of vital body medicine-acupuncture, chakra medicine, homeopathy, etc. This is the stage of unconscious processing in which we use unlearned stimuli to generate uncollapsed possibility waves at the vital and supramental (which guides the vital) levels; but we, in our ego, don't have the ability to choose among the possibilities.

We wait for supramental intelligence to descend and create the same kind of revolution at the feeling level as the creative insight at the mental level does for mental thinking. The net effect of the quantum leap, the revolution, will be the coming into existence of new vital blueprints and programs to help consciousness to rebuild the diseased organ and programs for its carrying out the vital functions. Since our feelings are related with the functioning of the programs that run the organs, as the vital programs begin to run smoothly, there will be an unblocking of the feeling at the appropriate chakra corresponding to what was once the diseased organ. This unblocking of feeling at a chakra comes with such force that it is called *the opening of a chakra.* For example, if cancer at the vital level is healed in this way, the heart chakra will open. And, indeed, this is like the samadhi or ah-ha experience of inner or outer (mental) creativity. It is transformative. If the heart chakra opens this way, our heart is not only open for romantic love, but also to universal compassion.

Now, the final stage of the creative process - manifestation. As in mind-body healing, manifestation is not complete with only the rebuilding of the physical representation (software) needed for proper functioning of the organ(s) involved. After the remission has taken place, the patient has to try to bring to manifestation the transformative universal compassion towards all. Otherwise, the heart energy will contract once again with disastrous consequences. In other words, when supramental heeds your call and teaches you a new trick, you take the lesson seriously and try to live it as far as possible.

Similarly, quantum healing of the vital diseases at any chakra opens that chakra and egoic expressions of feelings are transformed into universal expressions. When we creatively heal a root chakra disease, our feelings of competitiveness and fear transform into confident friendliness and courage respectively. Quantum healing of a sex chakra disease transforms the energies of sexuality and lust into respect for the self and others. In the same way, quantum healing at the navel lifts us from false pride and unworthiness to true self-worth. At the throat chakra, quantum healing transforms the feelings of frustration and egoic freedom of speech to real freedom of self-expression. Quantum healing of the third eye, transforms egoic confusion and ordinary clarity into intuitive supramental understanding. Finally, if a crown chakra disease is healed by a quantum leap, the leap will take us from the usual crown chakra preoccupation with the physical to an identity that includes the subtle as well.

Creativity of the Vital-Physical Body for the Well Person

Chakras are the places where we feel vital energy movements associated with the programs that run the functions of the important organs of our body. Of course, we identify with these movements as they become conditioned in our vital being, giving us a vital persona. For the navel, the heart, and the brow, at each chakra, we may even have a vital ego-persona, associated with our habit patterns of feeling there. There must even be a preconscious for the vital experience at these chakras- a few milliseconds gap between the quantum self and the ego experiences. Creativity of the vital/physical body for a well person is creative movement of vital energy beyond the conditioned movements of the vital physical ego/persona.

The creative process is *do-be-do-be-do*. Now suppose we do this practice, not with thoughts, but with feelings. Let's be specific and work on a heart chakra feeling-romance. I am concentrating on it, at the same time being relaxed about it with or without the object of my romance. Tantra gets its name of "left-handed path" because the practitioners often engage this practice with the romantic partner in the act of sexual embrace. It is very difficult to transcend the need for orgasm, the habitual expression of sexuality. If we succeed in side- swiping the movement of vital energy to the third navel chakra for collapsing, and continue looking at the energy with the intention of collapsing it in the heart, a time comes when we are dancing with the quantum self of a new creative expression of romance, universal romance or unconditioned love; we have entered the preconscious. If we stay in this dance for a while, sooner or later, we fall into the quantum self of supramental insight of new meaning and a universal feeling of unconditional love.

Feelings of vital energy, as we have mentioned before can be felt as currents or tingles or warmth, or just expansion of consciousness at the chakras specially, with a little practice. This creative feeling of unconditional love is felt as a current rising from the root chakra (or sex chakra). This rising energy is called *the awakening of Kundalini Shakti in tantra.* Kundalini means coiled up and Shakti means energy, vital energy. Poetically put, this energy is coiled up at the root chakra where it stays available but no collapse is possible (the metaphor is that of the physical potential energy of a coiled up spring). Once in a while, spontaneously, the potential energy transforms into kinetic energy, moving this way and that way, but those movements just add to the confusion people have about the vital energy domain. Indeed, many people seem to suffer when their kundalini exhibits such haphazard movements. Therefore, the adequate preparation beforehand should be mandatory. The Kundalini awakening experience on the other hand is directed movement. The process seems to create a new pathway; the energy is experienced to rise along this new pathway, in a straight channel along the spine, giving the practitioner an intense feeling of timeless universal love that has transformative value. That is, one has the opportunity to transform if one carries through the manifestation stage of creativity.

The tradition says that if the kundalini rises in one's experience from the root chakra following a new channel along the spine all the way to the crown chakra, then the Kundalini may be totally awakened. The control of vital energy movements becomes easy without effort.

In quantum science this would amount to collapsing the coiled-up energy at the lower chakras all the way at the 6th brow chakra. This is then an awakening of supramental intelligence using the vital-physical domain of experience.

Not only does creative vital energy movements authenticate our 'aha' experience, for example, shaking movements can be used to help the creative process itself. The spiritual teacher Rajneesh (later called Osho) used to teach a vital energy meditation; when we examine it, it is found to be a do-be-do-be practice just like in thought but involving vital energy, see below . And this is the same creative process except you have to involve vital energy movement and watch your energy. The practices called Chi Gong or Tai Chi are practices of do-be-do-be- do as well. The pranayama breathing practice with gaps called kumbhaka of holding the breath for a few seconds after both inhaling and exhaling is also a do-be-do-be-do practice.

Creativity and Chakra Psychology

If you are an average Westerner, you know little about the chakras and pay little attention to your visceral feelings. Your brain circuits are active; they and your environmental upbringing determine much of your behaviour. You have grown up being guided by the mind and finding security anyways you can from your physical situation: a good house, a good job, lots of money, and oh yes, a great car. If you have these things, your mind says you are "superior;" you feel sanguine that this is true even in others' eyes; after all you all belong to the same culture. If you don't have physical security, of course, you feel "inferior". This affects how you experience the interaction with another person, a challenge to your homeostasis.

The reason to explore the root chakra with creativity is straightforward: creativity enables you to realise that your real sense of security comes from your capacity to maintain attentive feeling of vital energy at the root chakra. The mental/cultural superiority/inferiority dynamic no longer apply. When potential danger approaches, you pay positive attention to the root chakra.

How do you apply creativity to open a chakra? The creative process used is always the same, do-be-do-be- do. For a starter you can try that four stage Rajneesh meditation that led me (Amit) to my first clear kundalini awakening experience: 1) shake while standing paying attention to vital movements; 2) standing meditation on the movement at the chakras; 3) closed eye slow dancing; and 4) sitting meditation on the chakras.

The techniques of pranayama, certain advanced yoga poses, and Tai Chi are also do-be-do-be-do practices and carried out diligently with the five I's - inspiration, Intention, Intuition, Imagination, and Incubation - will lead to the sixth I of Insight, which in this case is the awakening of kundalini. The optimal functioning of all three highest chakras - throat, brow, and crown, has to do with vital creativity - sublimation of root and sex chakra energy to collapse at the level of higher chakras.

There is also *Kapalabhati (pranayama of radiant skull)* that deserves special mention. This one is specifically acting on purifying the abdominal brain and Manipura navel chakra, so that lower chakra energies can freely rise to the brow chakra and clean up the mind.

Sit comfortably and start by taking in a small inhalation, and then practice forced exhalation of breath, using only your stomach muscles. Practice this between 20-40 times a minute. When this exercise is done properly, you will experience a few moments of breathlessness when you stop. Take your time to return to normal breathing. Notice that when you are without breath, you are also without thought. This thoughtless state - a state of unconscious being - makes way for quantum-self experiences and you may find a heightened sense of intuition.

What happens when kundalini-awakened people meet as strangers? Each person approaches the other as normal human beings responding to another human being in their well-defined roles. And each will respect the other's presence in the proper role and not become aggressive.

Why did Gandhi succeed in his non-violence movement? He was rooted. He neither had to fight nor resort to flight. Instead, he had creative control over his root chakra; he knew how to 'watch' his energy. To avoid the automatic fight-flight brain directed response to the adrenal glands, being able to pay attention to your root chakra is a viable option.

Energising of all chakras is a fundamental key for having perfect physical and mental health, for awakening the latent potentialities and for accomplishing an accelerated integration. The main thing is optimising the function of all organs at the level of the chakras. Together with Valentina, we will present below a few elements about the significance of this, both from scientific and esoteric perspectives.

Root Chakra (Muladhara)

This is, metaphorically speaking, the "battery" of the being, a foundation of the edifice of our physical-vital being. Ancient Yogic texts state that at this level we find the mysterious *kundalini* power, the potential for cosmic fusion.

The intuition of the ancient yogis was right. There is no tangled hierarchy at the organs of this chakra, so the root/Muladhara chakra energy indeed remains coiled up metaphorically speaking, remains uncollapsed. In animals, it gets some expression through the mid brain, where mammals have a self. In humans with a neocortical self dominating everything, this mid-brain self becomes unconscious.

However, as we become aware of higher chakras energy centers in the body, muladhara chakra coiled up energy can collapse at the navel and the heart, even at the brow chakra. Here, collapsing means energy moves up and transmutes into a higher chakra energy. In other words, quantum science says some chakras have tangled hierarchies and we speak of such selves at the level of third - manipura, fourth - anahata, and the sixth - agnya chakra.

Sexual Chakra (Swadhisthana)

In the mammals, this chakra coordinates the instincts (hunger, thirst, sex, sleep, etc) when expressed at the mid brain where animals have a self; for us humans, these instinctual functions are unconscious.

The energies specific to Swadhisthana Chakra are: pleasure, sensations, duality. There are a lot of taboos and dogmas around sexuality and pleasure, in the past and nowadays. On the other hand, Tantra shows that the state of satisfaction induced by intense pleasure has exceptional spiritual valences, as long as the energies at the level of Swadhistana Chakra are perfectly controlled and sublimated, collapsing at the level of the heart or even further up. To achieve this, of course, there has to be love in the practicing couple as a starting point. Then this energy can be integrated (transmuted) and sublimated (collapsed) into higher energies as it moves up and collapses at one of the higher chakras with self-identity.

When sex chakra energy rises to the mid brain and collapses there that's when people become sexually aggressive (although more or less unconsciously). The opposite occurs when the stimulus takes our attention away from the sex chakra. (Example: when you make love and someone enters the room, most civilised men would lose erection.)

When blockages appear at the level of Swadhisthana chakra, this can reflect in time in the physical body as diseases related to sexual function, but also to the heart (example: cysts, fibromas, impotence, frigidity).

The energies corresponding to Swadhisthana chakra, when they find expression in the higher chakras are connected to a wide range of emotions manifesting sensuality, creativity in many forms, capacity to enjoy for pleasure, playfulness, spontaneity and adaptability, especially at the social level.

The Navel Chakra (Manipura)

In the human being it coordinates ambition, ego, will-power, dynamism, expansion, violence; part of these functions is taken over by the mid-brain; when we regain partial control, there is a tendency for narcissism, ego and individuality. This narcissist aspect makes some people into dominators, into using their power for subduing others to do according to their own exacerbated egotistic will.

Only when the Manipura chakra opens in conjunction and harmony with the heart chakra and higher, the positive side of the Hara is realised. There is a process here of crystallising the life guiding principles of the movement of consciousness; this is why those who have a strong development of this chakra are the people that follow ethical principles in life and have self-confidence, will power and inner fortitude as factors for achieving their goals or of following certain life principles. This makes people who have this center harmoniously activated to be powerful leaders and in certain cases it enables them to evolve faster than others.

One of the most important tasks of Manipura Chakra in the human being's energetic system is to overcome inertia, to remove tendencies towards stagnation, self- indulgence, laziness, ignorance. This is the level where consciousness begins to wake up and to have glimpses manifested through aspirations and decisions, which are followed with firmness. For most people, the hardest thing is to start an action. At the beginning of an action, inertia is at its maximum, but once the beginning is done, the energies start to circulate and the results appear with less effort. This is why the Manipura Chakra is the center that ensures our ability to overcome the difficult moment before every beginning, and in this way paying attention to it we can act efficiently most of the times. In the same way, the Manipura Chakra is what ensures our exit from bad situations; it helps to unblock apparently "immovable" states of stagnation and inertia, and furthermore it produces the initiation of transformation processes. When a firm decision followed by fast action is necessary, attending to the Manipura Chakra is the solution. All tendencies to postpone and indulge are promptly eliminated by the dynamic energies at the Manipura Chakra.

Heart Chakra (Anahata)

At the conditioned level, the heart chakra is about romantic love. When creatively opened further, it leads to the capacity of compassion and other forms of unconditional love, forgiveness, selflessness. An open heart is related to even high aesthetics.

The role of the forth chakra, Anahata chakra, is to harmonise what is up (which is more and more transpersonal) with what is down (personal), in the following sense: heart chakra is where we become aware of other people; thus it balances Manipura chakra, assuring expansion of consciousness towards others while attending to oneself. Whereas the first 3 chakras are entirely individual and are used that way under mainly the control of the brain and partially of the self of the manipura chakra, the self at the heart chakra, even in its conditioned modality, is about expansion of consciousness to include the other. In this sense, it harmonises what is below and above, it is the junction.

By awakening the ability to love and compassion, we can say that materialism meets spirituality and in this way humanness appears in us. At the level of Anahata chakra we have the first experience of awakening a self-consciousness, not as an expression of an individual will affirmed through the actions we do, but in the form of the fundamental feeling of to be, to expand in the sense of including (another person).

Throat Chakra (Vishuddha)

The throat chakra is the chakra of expression. Our culture innately knows. Freedom of speech is probably the most cherished freedom; and ultimately freedom is about freedom to create. Where is free speech located? At the throat. When you feel restrained to speak your mind, you inadvertently cover your mouth. Body language again. There is no self identity at the throat chakra; there is no tangled hierarchy. So we have options: to express in the service of me, to express in the service of love, or to express in the service of the mind.

Chakra psychology links the throat chakra with the sex chakra. Indeed, who has not noticed that during the creative flow in the manifestation stage in which the throat chakra is a major actor, there is also a tendency of sexual excitement. It is because both the sexual energy and the expressive energy are at the service of me, both energies are being collapsed at the navel. Not only do we sublimate the sexual energy, we transform it and maintain attention on the throat chakra regardless. In this way, when both collapses at the brow chakra, we express with meaning and passion both.

The problem with this usual operation of the throat chakra is that it is still under the control of the mental self of the 6th chakra. It serves the intellectual mind. Only when the brow chakra fully opens making room for intuition (see below), the 5th chakra serves the soul.

This is the case with most genius artists, the specific energies of Vishuddha chakra are serving their soul, making their work a source of inspiration for those who are able to perceive the refined energies encrypted in these creations.

Brow Chakra (Agnya)

The brow chakra is the chakra of rational thinking. Agnya Chakra, generally, for normal people, processes the mind; however, if we pay attention and become aware of the energies at the chakra, all that vital energy adds juice and makes us passionate in mental thinking.

When this chakra opens, mainly due to the creative sublimation (collapsing) of sexual energy it becomes the chakra of intuitive thought. It now becomes the eye of intuition, usually called "the third eye". The associated feelings are now despair and satisfaction. "Seek and you shall find; and you will be troubled." When we explore an archetype, the archetype responds with an intuition and indeed, as it fades away, we are troubled, confused, in despair; we sense the truth value, feel it in our gut or heart, but cannot engage rational thinking to fully understand it. However, as we engage the creative process to explore the archetype and have an insight, satisfaction dawns. If additionally, we are able to bring the throat chakra to serve the awakened brow, our expressions achieve truth-value.

In India, when people do spiritual work, a time for a great many intuitive experiences, the third eye becomes so hot that people put sandalwood paste to soothe it. You may have seen Indian women wear a bindi on their forehead; the reason is the same at least traditionally speaking, intuition can be strong in women. Nowadays Indian women may be doing it because it is 'stylish'.

The harmonious creative activation of Agnya Chakra bestows upon the human being the awakening of their superior mental consciousness that we call "the soul" with characteristics like mental calm, focusing power, intelligence, power of mental synthesis, exceptional memorising capacity, and the power of profuse intuition. Also an integrated universal will power.

When integrated with the chakra at the mid-brain, the 6th chakra self gets to control the function of both the hypothalamus (which has control of the pituitary gland and all the hormones of the body) and the nervous structures that regulate the capacity of seeing, hearing, discriminating and memorising. Also, all the previous unconscious control that the brain had over the body is now under conscious control. Clearly, our major effort should go into awakening the 6th chakra to its fullest extent.

This is the key in understanding why the awakening of the brow chakra eventually opens our intuitive facility to the optimum. With mood swings under control, our capacity to be creative takes a quantum leap.

Only when the sixth chakra opens, are we capable of creatively engaging with more than one archetype to fruition within the span of one life. And as we do that, we integrate the archetypal dichotomies; we are ready for exploring the archetype of Wholeness in earnest.

One positive feeling associated with creative opening of the higher chakras is satisfaction. Whenever we open our heart or the throat or the brow, the chakra descent of consciousness has met with success and satisfaction arises. These episodes of satisfaction are fundamentally important for all human beings at any economic level. If we go through prolonged period of no satisfaction in life, we become depressed.

Psychologists worry that there is now an outbreak of depression so much so that it has become the third most prevalent chronic disease. The way quantum psychology looks at it, Prosac is only short-term support, if that. The long-term healing remedy of depression is satisfaction- readily obtainable through engagement of the creative process to cultivate the embodiment of the archetypes in us, especially the archetype of Wholeness. And rich, poor or middle class, everybody in a democratic society is entitled to it.

Crown Chakra (Sahasrara)

The biological function so far realised is to produce a body image including and integrating all the vital feelings. The organ is posterior superior parietal lobe. When energy moves into this chakra producing excess, we feel Wholeness - our identity is no longer restricted to the physical body but expands to include the subtle as well. If energy moves out, we feel disintegrated, disjoint.

The spiritual literature speaks very highly of the potentialities of this chakra. When this chakra fully opens, one develops an integrated identity with all of one's bodies - gross and subtle. This is a part what realising and embodying the archetype of Wholeness is about.

We don't know much about this chakra to engage much science except that it is located at the level of the parietal lobe, which has the capacity to make the homunculus, to make body image. The normal function is then body awareness. Whenever we see a mirror we take a look and check our body. If we don't find our body ok, we feel disoriented. Since the parietal lobe doesn't have or doesn't use the memory making capacity of its neurons, probably there is no self identity normally to be found here. However, it remains to be seen if spiritual exploration opening this chakra also leads to its own self identity.

The job to integrate this physical body image with the images of rest of our bodies - vital and mental- requires creativity! When we combine the force of both mental and vital creativity to this task, we open the door to supramental intelligence albeit in the service of soul- making.

As a side benefit, when this chakra opens, one develops the ability to dis-identify with the physical body producing the out-of-the-body experience, a capacity now much documented in some people. Don't be misled; people who have out-of-the-body experience do not necessarily develop the supramental intelligence about Wholeness.

Chapter 14

Integrating Sexuality and Love: The Quantum Version of Tantra

Direct exploration of an archetype takes fundamental creativity. The creative process of fundamental creativity is a little different from that of situational creativity. It does have six stages:

1. Inspiration, Intention, Intuition
2. Preparation
3. Unconscious processing
4. Do-be-do-be-do
5. Sudden aha insight of certain knowledge
6. Manifestation and flow

You notice, there is no more need for any consultation with a guru after your insight or any "try it and see". Fundamental creativity comes with certain knowledge of a quantum leap. You've already had the experience of quantum leap in situational creativity; you know how it feels like, feeling in the gut or heart. You are not going to be fooled.

In the manifestation stage, YOU manifest the insight TO MAKE A NEW YOU, a transformed you – actually to REMIND you of You. That makes knowledge into wisdom - lived knowledge.

When it comes to a specific archetype for exploring inner creativity, I (Amit) have personal experience of fulfillment with only one archetype - the archetype of Love. (I am still at the manifestation stage for the archetype of Wholeness as well as the archetype of Truth.) It so happens that Love and Wholeness are also Valentina's main archetypes of exploration.

Inner Creativity in Relationships

While acting, we wear masks and assume someone else's identity to explore and gain insight about our own masks of self-image. In relationship, we also have the opportunity to be in somebody else's shoes but more subtly.

The problem is, our ego thrives in homeostasis. This includes not only our own habits and character patterns, but also the tendency to manipulate others in relationship into the mould of our own perception. And if we allow movement in a relationship, it is often a horizontal movement within the contexts defined by our own ego. Breaking through these tendencies is a creative challenge, and the kind of creative acts that penetrate such an impasse and restore fluidity to frozen or static relationships has within them the capacity to catapult us beyond ego. In other words, personal growth in relationship is inner creativity.

Women's spirituality traditionally has always emphasised on relationships. And thanks to the women's liberation movement and, more recently, the men's movement and the work of such people as the poet Robert Bly, the demanding "R" word is no longer anathema to men, even in the West.

There are many kinds of relationships that we live and all of them afford us opportunities for exploring archetypes. Below, let's take the archetype of Love and examine how intimate relationship can act as a catapult for discovering love.

Preparation: From Sex and Romance to Commitment

Because of the instinctual brain circuits, our sexuality is aroused easily and often by a variety of stimuli. When we are teenagers and these feelings are unfamiliar we become confused about our sexuality. Most societies have a taboo against educating the young about sexuality. In some spiritual societies, the idea of celibacy is introduced for the young. Unfortunately, this is often done without much guidance as to why or how. The original idea could have been good: remain celibate until you discover romantic love when you will no longer be confused about the creative potential of your sexuality (beyond procreation). Without any avenue for such education, how is the confusion going to go away?

If a teenager goes into sex without understanding the creative potential and purpose of sex (we don't talk about "the birds and the bees" reproductive aspect of sex here that is generally taught in schools as sex education), he or she will blindly respond to the brain circuits and look upon sexuality as a gratification, as a vehicle for a unique kind of intense pleasure. Since the fulfilment of sexual pleasure for a male with a partner raises vital energy to the third chakra associated with the navel-self identity with the physical body, a sense of personal power enters the equation. Hence for males, it is common to think of "sexual conquests" in connection with sex that is not associated with romantic love. Recall that sex in romantic love raises the uncollapsed sexual energy of the second chakra all the way to the heart chakra; that is, the actualisation of the feeling at the second chakra occurs in association of the self of the heart.

In the Western world, the pattern that has developed over the last few decades, at least for men, is this early conditioning of sex for power. Women, thanks to some protective ("conservative") parents, are somewhat exempt from this trend although that is rapidly changing. What happens when you eventually discover a partner with whom your heart chakra resonates? You enter the romantic love relationship, but your habit of conquest remains, just temporarily abated. The romance eventually runs out; it does that sooner or later because of yours and everybody's tendency to habituate every new experience, the sex-hormone oxytocin (popularly called "the love-hormone") becomes scarce in the bloodstream. Naturally, the sex-for-power tendency returns. You then have a choice. You can return to 1) conquesting; 2) look for another romantic partner; or 3) go deep in the existing relationship to explore its creative potential. If you take the derring-do of the third option in stride, new questions will come up: Can you love without being driven by the love-hormone? Can you love unconditionally?

Why the social custom of a man being the one who asks his romantic partner to enter marriage? To enter marriage is to change the equation of sex: I will commit to change my pattern of using sex for power to using sex always to make love. Which means you are committing always to allow the energy to rise to the heart after a sexual encounter, and that way allow yourself to become vulnerable to your partner. Marriage is a commitment to make love, not war (to conquest). Can you handle it?

Actually, it is even more complicated than that; this vital body agreement concurrently has to find agreements between the mental bodies of the partners as well. For mental bodies of a couple, the individual ego conditionings are very deep; in the arenas of overlap of ego activity there will be territoriality, and competitiveness will emerge and bring the energy down from the heart chakra to the navel chakra once again resulting in a return to narcissism. You may have heard the joke. A man says to his wife when she expressed dissatisfaction with their marriage: "I don't get it. Your job is to make me happy. I am perfectly happy. So what's the problem?"

The competitiveness and other negative emotions will relent only when we begin to intuitively glimpse that it is possible to surrender the negative emotions to the positive energy of love.

A Calvin and Hobbs cartoon describes the situation with the narcissistic tendency of the ego perfectly. Calvin says, "I am at peace with the world. I'm completely serene." When pressed by Hobbes, he clarifies, "I am here so everybody can do what I want." From this place, we can love only magnanimously, from the superior level in a simple hierarchical relationship and feed the narcissism of the ego. But this is not love and it only leads to isolation. When you become aware of your loneliness, in spite of having friends and partners, you should begin to inquire why you are lonely, why you do not feel loved, and why, in truth, you are unable to give unselfish love either.

It is then that you know that the time has come to be serious about engaging the creative process of discovering love, you have passed the entrance requirement, motivation. Motivation for a monogamous relationship.

I (Amit) know; I went through all this. I had a wife who challenged me to love from the heart, not the cerebral love that looks for multiple partners to service ego's narcissism. It took me some years but eventually I took up the challenge.

The next step is preparation, unconscious processing, and do-be-do-be-do. And this, to begin with is to engage situational creativity. I read books, looked at what other people say about rekindling romance; I researched all of these teachings to generate a lot of divergent thinking. And then I relaxed; I engaged unconscious processing and do-be-do-be-do following that.

Insight came with the quantum leap; I manifested the insight in my living. And I really thought I loved my wife unconditionally; this is it. I felt committed to her. I was no longer needing to look for other female attention. I was happy. When a physicist friend's dancer wife asked me, "What is your biggest creative accomplishment?" I said without hesitation, "I discovered how to love my wife." Imagine my surprise when a couple of years later, my wife left me. "You are incapable of giving me what I need," were her parting words.

Double-Slit Processing in the Exploration of Love

How does one include the other in making decision on living, satisfy the partner's need as well as one's own needs? A spiritual teacher told me, "Amit, learn to take responsibility for others." How do I do that? The answer came in a few years just when I needed it, when I remarried, and again after a few years the romantic juices were threatening to run out.

Our conditioning does not allow incoming stimuli to evoke a variety of responses in our mind-brain-vital body-physical body complex. Instead our conditioning acts like a slit that permits us to process the stimulus in the same conditioned perspectives that we have used before. It is very much like the case of the electron passing through a single slit before falling on a fluorescent screen. It appears right behind the slit, only a little blurring of its image due to diffraction gives away the secret that the electron is still a wave of possibility and not an entity of complete fixity of a point.

If we pass the electron through both slits of a double slitted screen (fig. 3), every electron wave becomes two waves of possibility which interfere. If we put a photographic plate to catch the electrons, they will arrive at some places adding constructively; in between places, they will arrive in opposite phase and destroy each other out. The net effect is what physicists call *an interference pattern*. Notice how the possibility pool of the electrons is enhanced enormously; the electron is able to arrive at so many places on the photographic film now.

This is the magic of having an intimate relationship whom you want so much to love and cherish that for every stimulus you not only allow your belief system to sift the responses through but your partner's belief system (as per your educated theory of the other's mind) as well making her/him into a double slit for unconscious processing. Is the phase relationship required to create an interference pattern preserved? If you so intend, it must. That is my experience.

In this way, having a committed intimate relationship with the intention of taking responsibility for the other's needs as well as yours is like creating a double slit to sift all your incoming stimuli through in this way enhancing your possibility pool for unconscious processing. The truth is, you may not yet consciously recognise your partner's contexts for looking at things; but your unconscious is already considering them, hence your intention alone can make the change. Your possibility pool to choose from is now much bigger, and chances are better that new possibilities for creativity are already there for the quantum consciousness to enter the picture and choose.

Psychologists would call the above a part of empathy training. It works so much better if we allow unconscious processing and most importantly nonlocality as I discussed earlier.

Even all that may not be enough, is not enough. Today career conflicts raise their ugly head; agendas become different. There are so many ways to move apart in a relationship! Two questions come: 1) Is there any built-in dynamic between a man and a woman that holds them together in the creative journey? 2) Is there any way to guarantee that there will be new possibilities in the pool to resolve conflicts?

Male-Female Polarity and Its Role in a Relationship

To be in love forever is one of the most widespread aspirations that we entertain in our souls, whether we are conscious about it or not. It goes beyond education, gender, nationality and dogmatic beliefs - religious or scientific, for it is one of life's greatest experiences and makes us feel that life's worth living.

I (Valentina) see so many people suffering in intimate relationships these days. Aren't such relationships the best ground for experiencing love and all its wonders? And since in one way or another we want it so much, why is love so easy to get and once you get it, so hard to maintain? The root of this apparently paradoxical situation can be found in one of the fundamental aspects of human life and one of the main principles of the love relationship. Without it we wouldn't fall in love, we wouldn't be attracted to another human being, and we wouldn't even be able to have a relationship. It's called *polarity* and it lies at the foundation of the Secrets of Attraction. What is Polarity? Polarity is the relation that appears in the presence or manifestation of two opposites or contrasting principles or tendencies.

Remember what it's like in the beginning of a romantic relationship – it's an intensely overwhelming, effervescent state in which our hearts feel so open, we are powerfully attracted to each other, erotically charged and capable of loving unconditionally. This is the moment when polarity in the relationship can be seen in all its glory ... but only by an external observer. For the two people in love, the amazing effects of this game cover its mechanisms completely and make them blind towards the very source (engine) of their delicious passion and attraction.

The consumer attitude combined with ignorance towards this very powerful mechanism and ignorance about the brain's role, lead to the gradual deterioration of the initial, intense flame. This is why this ideal period of the beginning often comes to a premature and tragic end. I know it's hard to believe this, but we are the ones who via ignorance, unconsciously kill it just like the incorrect use of an engine eventually leads to its destruction.

Happily, according to the way I (Valentina) learnt as part of the esoteric tantric system, things don't have to be like this. The secret of attraction in a relationship is rooted in a continuous and consciously maintained effervescent polarity. This results in having effervescent dynamism – a strong play in the game between masculine and feminine in the relationship. The polarity in our relationship can be modified through a conscious approach, giving us control over the relationship's dynamism itself. And this has powerful repercussions throughout our entire life.

Tantra sees the entire creation as a result of the dynamic interaction of the two poles–immanent and transcendent, masculine and feminine, Yang and Yin. The clearest expression of this dynamic reality, and the one which is closest to us, can be seen in the game between the man and woman, the masculine and feminine, in a polar couple relationship.

At the core of a polar couple relationship is Love and the power that it generates. Love gives experience that reason cannot understand and motivates our hearts to grow and reach out to one another beyond the self-assumed boundaries of our egos. The very engine of the attraction that keeps the couple relationship in the flow of their love is *THE GAME OF POLARITY* – the game between masculine and feminine. It is what gives life and support to everything. In Tantra, it is known as the game between *Shiva and Shakti* – the universal masculine and feminine.

Attraction is empowered by polarity. This is an esoteric key that can explain many things throughout our life. If we want attraction, the key is to find intense polarity - opposites attract. This empowers the life of the couple relationship and it also empowers all the phenomena we want to experience within the relationship and within our individual lives. Intense polarity will increase the speed of transformation as well as the capacity to control it.

Quite simply, from this perspective the secret to a long-lasting and intensely alive relationship is keeping up the game of polarity. Empowered by a strong polarity the manifestations of love are potent and stable, the two lovers become emotionally generous and want to share their love with the world.

When polarity diminishes, attraction decreases, problems amplify and deepen, transformation slows down and life loses its colours. We've all had this experience in one way or another – suddenly we discover things in the other one that were always there, but now we cannot accept them anymore, we cannot transfigure them. Usually, the man gets lazy and the woman gets superficial and the super intense battery that was created in the beginning is now practically dead. What to do when this happens?

I checked this out, on my own "skin", while I was living all day long together with my lover, and all my life was revolving around him. Being all the time together, losing the healthy centeredness (and thus one's natural feminine or masculine mystery), can be indeed very damaging even for the status of personal health, as well for the relationships' state of health - and explained by this fact of losing the state of polarity in the respective couple.

The good news is that the initial spark of love can be brought back as often as the two lovers want, if they know how to apply this knowledge of polarity and constantly reignite the flame of the relationship until you love each other like when you were teenagers. Regaining the feelings that otherwise appeared to be long gone is a gift of youth that we can give to each other and to our relationship. It is perhaps the most important gift to ever give.

In order to reignite the passion, you have to recharge the battery – to restore and even increase polarity. You do this by emphasising your differences, not compromise them. Sure, you fight, but you let the unconscious process it the quantum way and come up with creative resolution.

The effects are wondrous: we discover that the love we have for each other is not dead, but just weakened by lack of power and buried beneath the rubble produced by the mind. And with the newly restored power, our love rises again on the sky of our soul, soaring above all problems and even conquering new horizons. This gives the feeling of rebirth of the intense love that is similar to what existed in the beginning.

When you decrease polarity because you want peace of mind, you flatten the battery of creative power through lack of use and all that was based on that power will diminish and disappear, not because it's not needed or wanted but because it's out of power. This is one of the best kept secrets about relationships. A relationship is a battery of power which can be "recharged" again and again, if we know how, if we know about polarity. Knowing and applying this equips us to be able to have a long- lasting, deeply fulfilling, intensely happy relationship.

I had people in my health practice with a wrong understanding of the difference between gender complementarity vs gender equality. Even if it is normal that the two poles of a power unit are fundamentally different without being wrong, we tend to forget this in our daily existence today. Failing to understand the role of polarity and the complementarity that exists between men and women leads to a lack of dynamism in relationships, lack of attraction, and ultimately the inability to have a relationship. Underlining the polar difference between men and women is not conolict really, but a complementarity that naturally exist between men and women who are in love. Men and women are different, neither is better than the other.

Instead of making an effort to understand these differences, thus to understand each other and our polar role in love's special situation, we have opted instead to try to level the playing field. Now there is almost an obsession with gender equality that is mistakenly leading to universal gender neutrality. Unisex culture pervades Western societies as a reaction to what we see in other cultures where one gender suppresses the other in an attempt to deal with the powerful attraction generated by the natural occurrence of balanced polarity. We unconsciously tend to eliminate the very source of power of our life in an attempt to take out all the negative effects of power. And the problems are extending when we try to solve all the side effects of this erroneous focus of the attention.

There is nothing wrong in acknowledging the fundamental differences between man and woman, and to cultivate these differences in a way that gives the right position to both of them when the situation is appropriate. This is also a far better solution to gender inequity and will also give men and women the lessons that they need to learn instead of giving them reasons to hide most of these needed life lessons behind a misunderstood gender problem.

Then the sum of all individual consequences of these decisions make a bigger problem: a society without polarity; without polar tension that naturally occurs between the two genders we create a society without power, without purpose, and one that can be easily controlled by all kind of agendas.

Of course, as a society, we do need to worry about that one vile aspect of human society - the tendency to form simple hierarchy. Even in a love relationship, without transformation, people are simply ego-personas, each with simple hierarchies to protect. Naturally, each promptly tries to manage the relationship with a simple hierarchical domination of the other. Over historical times, men have been more successful in the domination game. Modern women's "liberation" movement was necessary to release women worldwide from this subservience to age-old simple hierarchy with men dominating women. And then we have the pitfall of ho-hum gender equality of political correctness!

Is there a quantum way to define relationship between two people that respects polarity but does not succumb to the pitfall of gender equality via political correctness? There is. The quantum answer is *tangled hierarchy.*

Practicing Tangled Hierarchy with Your Partner and Inviting Quantum Consciousness to Resolve Your Conflicts

At this stage, your relationship has to take a turn towards transforming from a simple hierarchy to a tangled hierarchy.

Look at the Escher picture of the Drawing Hands (fig. 14). In the picture the tangled hierarchy is created because the left hand is drawing the right, and the right hand is drawing the left, but you can see that this is an illusion. Behind the scene, Escher is drawing them both. When from your study of the quantum measurement you truly have taken the quantum leap of understanding that the reality of your manifest consciousness, the subject-hood of the subject-object partnership arises from the quantum choice and actualisation from an undivided quantum consciousness, you also have identified the source of your tangled hierarchy you are trying to emulate - the unmanifest quantum consciousness. You have to relegate authority to that One. How do you shift your authority from the manifest to the unmanifest, even temporarily?

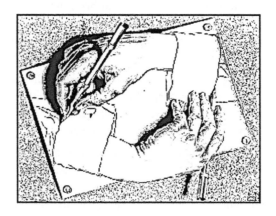

Fig. 14. Esher's Drawing Hands (artist's rendition)

It is in this phase of discovery that if your love partner is also your intimate enemy can become a huge boon.

The movie, *The Wedding Date,* is not a great movie by any means, but to my satisfaction it has one thing right. At some point in a fighting scene between the partners of the romantic couple, the hero said to the heroine something to the effect, "I want to marry you, because I'd rather fight with you than make love with another person." To practice unconditional love, it is important to recognise your love partner shamelessly as "the intimate enemy." The behavioural advice is to use reason to settle the differences that cause fighting ("renegotiating your contract") but unfortunately this amounts only to suppressing emotions. Or if emotions break out anyway, the behavioural advice is to leave the scene, to not to let things "get out of hand," or "to kiss and make up," which is usually a pretension until sexual instinct takes over. These are perhaps good advices for people who are not ready for unconditional love. For you, the inner fundamental creative, your challenge is to love your partner in spite of your differences. And when these differences cause a fight, then so be it, remain in the fight explicitly or implicitly until a quantum leap takes place or until the situation become unbearable at your present stage of personal emotional maturity. Conflicts are guaranteed to bring new possibilities in your pool for processing and who can process the new but quantum consciousness/God? Gradually, we become capable of waiting out unresolved conflicts for longer and longer time.

With this strategy, sooner or later, you will fall into a creative aha, a quantum leap, a discovery of the "otherness" of the other (to use sociologist Carol Gilligan's very appropriate language), not unconsciously, but consciously.

The practice, to hold unresolved conflicts longer and longer until resolution comes from higher consciousness is a difficult practice, but the rewards of its manifestation stage after the creative insight that takes place are enormous. The conditions that we impose on our love now can fall away with practice and love can blossom into unconditional, objective love. Objective love because the love of quantum consciousness is objective.

And then we have a choice. So all that polarity is a gift to us for the exploration of the tangled hierarchical relationship!

Once we can love unconditionally, sex is a choice. We do not need it to make love. The manifestation of unconditional love also means that you cannot make a brain circuit of it. Anything coming from a brain circuit is a conditioned pattern as liberating as it may be. Instead you do something even better.

You try to live the tangled hierarchy with your love-partner. What it means is you live your relationship with intuition as your guide in the main. The brain circuits you make will further contribute to your soul-making.

And eventually you will do this for relationships with anyone that comes in your sphere of living simply because you find that you cannot do otherwise.

In this regard, here is a wonderful poem by Victor Hugo:

Man and Woman

The man is the most elevated of creatures,
The woman is the most sublime of ideals.
God made for the man a throne; for the Woman an altar.
The throne exalts; the altar sanctifies.
The man is the brain; the Woman is the heart.
The brain creates light; the heart creates love.
Light engenders; love resurrects.
The Man is strong because of his reason.
The Woman is invincible through her tears.
Reason is convincing; tears are deeply touching.
The Man is capable of all heroism.
The Woman - of all sacrifice.
Heroism ennobles; sacrifice brings all that is sublime.
The Man has supremacy; the Woman, intuition.
Supremacy represents strength.
Intuition represents righteousness.
The Man is a genius; the Woman, an angel.
Genius is immeasurable; the angel ineffable.
The man aspires towards supreme glory.
The woman aspires towards perfect virtue.
The Glory creates all that is great; the virtue, all that is divine.
The Man is a code; the Woman is a gospel.
A code corrects; the gospel perfects.

The Man thinks; the Woman dreams.
To think is to have a superior brain.
To dream is to have a halo on the brow.
The Man is an ocean, the Woman a lake.
The ocean has the adorning pearl; the lake, dazzling poetry.
The Man is a flying eagle; the Woman, a singing nightingale.
To fly is to conquer space; to sing is to conquer the soul.
The Man is a temple; the Woman a shrine.
Before a temple we uncover our head; before a shrine we kneel.
In short, the man is where earth ends. The woman is where heaven begins.

When we integrate the male and the female and live our relationships in tangled hierarchy we live in both earth and heaven; in other words, we can have our cake as well as eat it. We can enjoy our enlightenment.

Amit's Story

In conscious awareness, we can't respond to a stimulus in one way and the opposite way at once, but our unconscious can deal with opposites.

We love our intimate ones, but when our self-interest enters the picture and they oppose it, they become our enemies, have you noticed? You love and you hate; of course, not in the same response in conscious awareness. Creativity theorists say, try to do it at the same time and relax. Let your unconscious process the juxtaposition of love and hate at the same time!

Jesus advised something like this. "Love your enemy," he said. Pablo Picasso drew a picture of this, the Minotaur, (fig. 15), dagger and olive branch at the same time. The philosopher Hegel said the same thing: Put thesis and antithesis together, and watch the synthesis grow in you.

Fig. 15. Picasso's minotaur (artist's rendition)

It is so easy to talk, but how do I do this, process in my unconscious love and hate at the same time? One time, I was viciously arguing my case with my spouse about the subject of our frequent disagreement, my/our excessive travel which her body could not handle, when an idea struck me. I asked her for a bathroom break to which she nodded yes. I went to the toilet, closed the door and took a deep breath, and started an exercise: to bring the energy to the heart. After a few minutes of that, I went back to the argument and joined in as intensely as I could while simultaneously maintaining love in my heart. We did not have a resolution then, but this was a very constructive battle. The unconscious liked what I did. While I was listening to her, "being" in between my "doing," my unconscious was contributing new ideas to my conscious awareness.

Then soon, one day the insight came. It is one more quantum step further than empathy: I discovered the "otherness" of the other and got my message. You got to respect your lover's otherness and move towards tangled hierarchy in the relationship.

What I did not know at that time is that what I did is part of a Tantra practice as well. According to Vijnana Bhairava Tantra, one of the easiest ways to awaken the supramental is to be able to focus simultaneously on two opposite aspects of an archetype. In one of the following chapters, Valentina, who made me aware of this aspect, will describe this method in all its simplicity and efficiency.

To repeat: Our conscious mind is incapable of holding a thing and its opposite at once. I was able to hold opposites because I was using the heart and the mind both. If you are unable to do that remember this: Our quantum unconscious is multidimensional. If we manage to focus completely on two opposite aspects in the do phase of our creative practice, then in the be-phase, we fall into the quantum unconscious; when the quantum leap takes place, we discover the supramental archetype transcending the opposites.

What I also didn't know is this. See, there is no making a brain circuit of an archetypal insight; no words will describe it fully either. Ultimately it is changing your character: to engage not in a simple hierarchical relationship but in a tangled hierarchical relationship. And live authentic to your character.

In all my relationships as an adult, I had always put me first; the other, even a "loved" one was always secondary in my estimation. I saw through that now. Instead, love is to respect the other unconditionally; then tangled hierarchy; then the other and I become one - a self in which my end and her beginning becomes blurry.

Back to manifestation. My lack of respect for my wife expressed itself maximally in my attempt to manipulate her and get my way so surreptitiously, even engaging in white lies that obscured her ability to discern whether I was also protecting her self-interest. As a result, she would grant me the benefit of doubt and give in and become unhappy later.

And this giving in was really not suiting her. As I was getting older, and as she found it more and more challenging to accompany me on my travels due to her inability to cope with its inherent discomforts, her anxiety over my falling sick on the road gradually increased to the level of virtually neurosis. I decided to stop this manipulative behavior on my part. Serve her interest first. It was very hard.

I would manipulate her, then recognise it, come back and confess, and begin again. This happened a few times.

Then, one day, surprise of surprises. In the middle of a white manipulating lie, I became tongue-tied: I could not say it. I was amazed. I had lost the capacity for manipulation!

Transformation works with things like that! God is in the details. The new modus operandi does not always take care of numero uno as much as the old me would have liked, but it sure maximises both people's happiness in a relationship.

That's a major part of my story of how I learned unconditional love. There is more to come.

Chapter 15

Wholeness and I (Valentina)

I grew up in a small country in Eastern Europe, called Romania. I was born in a strongly opinionated family of doctors and priests, and in a communist country.

From a very early age I asked myself questions like: what is this life really about, what means freedom, what is healing and health, what happens after we die, what about love and all these intense vital energy manifestations that we have, thought and feelings? What about the human potential? Why there is so much suffering in this world? Why am I here?

I was a curious child. My family was quite well off, materially speaking, but my hunger was for more depth and understanding. There were also awakened within me *interesting* healing capacities and intuitions. Those traits were initially inexplicable for my father, who used to be quite a brilliant doctor. Eventually, he had to admit that there was more to know about human beings, and definitely human beings were more than just matter.

For example, at times, when I was placing my palms on painful areas of somebody and those symptoms were almost immediately released; or when I was dreaming of the next day questions on an exam paper; or when, after days of fasting with water only, I was extremely energetic and evermore clear; or to see me passionately working three days continuous shifts in a row in my emergency clinic, in a state of increasing dynamism and lucidity, I could see the struggle for a materially oriented doctor trying to accept such things happening right under his nose. Some things about me were happening not according to his manual and that was fun.

On my part, I inherited from him a lot of the determination to see things well done, with adherence to truth, and with courage and perseverance. Well, some stubbornness too.

My mother, a loving and compassionate person, probably had never lied or compromised what she knew (or felt) to be true. Indeed, a very sensitive and powerful woman in her own way, with a lot of intuitive capacity awakened. She had also specialised in the medical field. As a woman, naturally she was (still is) more accepting that there is more than what the eye sees in the world. She was often allowing herself to smile, pure like a child, and wonder about our human (especially healing) capacities. And she herself had quite some intuitions; she could, for example, often times, perceive various events or states people close to her were experiencing at far distance. Anyway, she never doubted her intuitions, she could accept that they were real.

I learnt from my mother the value of Goodness - she is very much at ease about very quickly forgiving and forgetting negative events. On the other hand, she was also trying to direct me towards to do with me having a so called "practical and normal" life (for which I was not so inclined). You know, get a stable job, ensure a pension, marry, have kids....

My parents love each other even if like most couples, had their relationship struggle due to their strong and different type of personalities. Life brought me a lot of opportunities and significant encounters in order to learn the importance of balance and harmony and pursue growth and inner alchemy through Love.

I was more of a rebel but a dedicated student of Life. Most times you would find me passionately devouring alomost any kind of books I could find. I was also assimilating school stuff very fast just to get back to my books. On the other hand, when I really wanted to do something which was not in my parents' agenda of approval (such as my yoga course that was seen like voodoo in those times of communist domination), I was literally jumping off the balcony to do it if I had to. The reward for following my heart was there always.

There was a deep spiritual call inside of me, whose voice has never stopped. I always felt protected and even guided towards the next steps of my integration, even in the most difficult and paradoxical periods of my life.

Not at all am I saying that my integration or journey is complete. The more I discover, understand and experience, the more I realise that I don't know much actually, that there is so much more to it. And I remain quiet and in peace, curious and open. The journey is so much worth it.

Speaking of journey, I have traveled a lot. Astral travels are also among my favourites, also the physical travels. Together with the great lessons they bring, comes another type of inner stability. I'm also getting used to living "at the limit". The propensity of pushing my own limits was always there.

Sometimes it is the other way around. Few years ago, while I was walking on the streets of Copenhagen, suddenly a state of expansion *hit* me *out of the blue* with this idea: *I am not going to places, but the places come to me.* Sounds strange? Still, it felt completely right to me, in a feeling of increasing expansion.

One of the most difficult questions I get is: where is your home? This question gets me easily in a Zen state. I realise more and more that actually my home is wherever I am.

Discovering Love and working through the dynamic of relationship was not an easy thing for me. Then again, Love is God's most fundamental energy, and we shouldn't miss the chance to discover it while living this life. It takes a lot of courage and honesty, but what is there to live for, if there is no Love? I discovered for myself love's tremendous and unique transformative value, and of course, I had to suffer through the pain in the process, the pain that heart vulnerability brings.

I have experienced love's healing and awakening power, the beauty and the brightness that it brings for a loving couple, especially when they consciously engage in spiritual growth. Whether there is physical distance or not. I am experiencing even now in my love relationship so much of all that overwhelming grace that we usually don't even intuit that it is possible to live in a life time. Love mirrors all your shadows but then it allows you to taste from the purest essence of reality, both manifest and transcendent. Then love manifests actually as a field, not limited to the one we love, but to all that is. Love in the pursuit of Wholeness is a path in itself. My mainly developed archetypes are Love and Wholeness. I will present more on this in my upcoming book written with Prof. Goswami, *Quantum Science of Love.*

As I grew up and embraced the art of medicine, studying and practicing various alternative branches as well, I naturally opened up towards spirituality in various forms – Christianity, Hinduism, Buddhism. I studied and put in practice in parallel for years in a row, spiritual traditions and practices, and integrative medicine methods in several countries. There was always something that was the same, a seed of Truth that was guiding my next step. I am grateful to have met, learned from and worked together with quite a number of rare exceptional souls of this planet, who are on their duty, serving the world with the highest intention of healing and awakening humanity.

I met Prof. Goswami in India in 2016. There was so much simplicity (although he was talking about very complex things), love, compassion, integrative wisdom, patient acceptance and common sense in his talk that I immediately felt the necessity and the naturalness of working together, complementarily. He was speaking my heart: about the awakening of the human potential, about healing ourselves and the world, about fulfilling our dharma. The integration of science and spirituality was an urge for me too, and there was no way I could have said No to his invitation to collaborate with him and his team.

From synchronicity to synchronicity, project after project, mirror after mirror, working together with Amit has been (and is) to me deeply healing, educational, and constantly supporting, exemplary and inspiring. Not always in complete harmony in thinking, sometimes there are hours and days of intense debates, but, interestingly enough, new paths open up for unconscious to process, and there, on the table, lies a new thing that reaches its integration. Sometimes right away, sometimes after months, but it's always there.

I used to be shy, intimidated about public speaking. I still am sometimes. Especially in the men (reason) dominated scientific circles which seem to force one to be.. more of a *man*. (I want to keep blossoming as a woman, first of all). Working with Prof. Goswami and with the people I came across has made me break through the speaking problem, because I hugely heed the need of people to heal, integrate, and awake. Their need moves deeply my heart, and I see that I have what to offer and contribute a great deal to people's transformation and healing.

Here are two of the most significant events in my life. They are quantum leaps, very much related with the fulfilment of the archetype of Wholeness and I present them here in the spirit of the book, otherwise I don't use to talk much about me. They may have some value for those familiar with the terms included in the description. I'm using some of the notes I wrote in my journal at those times, to help carry the message throughout.

Take in consideration the fact that Wholeness as an archetype is about integrating dichotomies. Both polarities of a dichotomy have substance. In self- realisation the two poles of the self that we experience melt into the unity, they don't have other existence besides unity, they are both illusory in some sense. While in Wholeness, when we are integrated, we are still in the expanded consciousness along with the archetype. We don't dissolve into the unity consciousness completely, certain amount of separateness remains. There is still the enjoyment of the archetype in its suchness for example.

One of the most valuable integrative education that I have gone through while in Europe – out of the Indian tradition, is the MahaVidya system. One of the 10 Cosmic Powers (aspects of the feminine creative divine aspects, pillars on which is built the entire creation) that this system emphasises upon, is *Tara*, the great cosmic power of compassion and divine grace. She is described both in the hindu and Tibetan buddhist tradition as the *saviour*, or the "star" who guides you through the foggy ocean of samsara; she simply takes you to the other shore. She is also *the mother of Boddhisattvas.* An energy and support that is very much needed nowadays.

This specific event occurred in July 2013, in Europe, in a meditation retreat. Just think of Grace. Whenever we say "quantum leaps", we say "Grace" as well. At that point, I was in a prolonged deep state of suffering and agony, which simply was hard to come out of in spite of all my efforts. I knew it had an important lesson for me - especially women know the feeling when the heart feels like "broken".

As the 7 days retreat started, I could simply feel, from one day to the other, lots of light, healing and inspirations, lots of intuitions about me and the universe. It felt like they were coming "out of the blue", without expectations. Echoes and reverberations of these messages were in my entire being, to the deepest levels, day and night. Not easy to describe those overwhelming states of completely unexpected Grace, of direct communion with Tara.

From the beginning of the camp, I could feel "something"high supporting me, as if Tara herself, in all her infinite power of manifestation, took me easily, softly and tenderly into Her heart (which was also my heart) and there She worked miracles. I have never experienced this much softness and unconditional loving motherly embrace.

The first acknowledgment of Her unsuspected presence inside of me, appeared on the 3rd day of the retreat, while, between meditations and hatha yoga practices, the Law of miracles was presented. The fact that Tara is present even in the darkest moments and places was mentioned, and that She shows us thus a great lesson: that in reality, we are never alone. This simple uttering stroked me with such immediacy! She literally started to strongly but in the same time softly, unfold within me, beginning with my heart, putting light on a situation that I had not even considered.

I was literally shown the inside of my heart, which was at that time mostly stoned and almost dead (the result of the suffering I was going through, no doubt) and the following situation. Somehow, in a proud and isolating way, I was not even considering asking for God's help, thinking I was not worthy of it, and not even hoping for someone or something to help. I was struggling unsuccessfully to allow Life within. When this insight happened, I felt like crashing down and losing my consciousness, like fainting. I was breathless, and I called for Her right away and realised in that very instant Her overwhelming presence in the form of a star made of white bright light which was instantly there, in me, with me. This was a huge 'aha' moment! I realised how much I have been longing for God, and a deep state of ecstatic trance of reunion appeared and continued deeper and deeper in me, as the days and nights went by.

I started to contemplate the world, the surroundings, the unfolding moments as they were, and a deep peace and allowance of what is took its place ever expanding within me. I was getting more and more literally ecstatic and out of the mode of separating things, defining them rigidly, or judging them.

The synthesis meditation at the end of the Tara retreat was again different. I was already in a natural and deep state of gratitude. She suddenly manifested Her grace in a form of a beautiful green bright light which surrounded me, uplifting and carrying me in a sudden deep ecstatic trance, where I was feeling light explosions and intense happiness not only in all the cells of the physical body but also a lot outside of it, in layers and layers. I felt that I hardly could contain that much happiness; it made me burst into laugh and tears simultaneously. The ecstatic state was expanding more and more and there was no more "me", nothing but pure cosmic bliss. I was light like a feather, not feeling at all my body as if it was made of ecstatic pure light I have never experienced ecstasy with that much beauty and peace.

This was a manifestation of divine Grace which healed my heart and made possible the first fundamental step towards Wholeness. Seeing Beauty in everything was also part of it.

Afterwards, it was so natural for me to focus and extinguish the occasional remaining doubting voice of the mind. Things "fell in place" and I started to live a beautiful simplicity, for about 3 months; this turned into blissful cosmic awareness, a constant call for a healthy, coherent and happy life with meaning. The constant perception was that of a sacred space and time with no boundaries and limitations, nor within nor without.

Nothing but pure existence, bliss and light. I felt as reborn in an absolutely miraculous way and bathed in pure condensed Grace. The marks on my heart were gone and the heart cracked open more and more. My relation with God was reestablished. My whole being became alive and although deeply happy and joyful, it remained overall in a state of contemplation of the beauty of the world and the magic of each moment. I have never seen with such thirst such amazing sunsets, and the sky and the air was never so alive and playful. Never were the flowers, trees, grass and animals around me so funny and sweet, nor the people so fantastic, and the smell of the air so wonderful, and my heart so peaceful and the silence so full and mysterious.

I was often experiencing now blissful periods of having no thoughts, and a deep, continuous and earth shaking gratitude to all that is, understanding and love of human nature and sorrow for the pain of the world and especially for the pain I caused to others while walking around stone hearted (this is what we actually do when we suffer, we also hurt others).

The simple feeling of being, only gratitude and amazement were left in me along with an increased lucidity. Something wide and mysterious was expanding in me and many times I was perceiving as if the outside world was moving or simply was sitting, simply existing within me. I was feeling as if the wind was blowing the tree's leaves inside of me; other things, animals or people, I was feeling all as part of me, as if they were inside of me. Small universes and worlds became wide and vivid for me and I was contemplating them in awe. The rhythm of life had changed. I felt full of amazement and gratitude that I am part of Tara, that I completely belong to God and that my home is pure light.

This was that particular week's experience. No alcohol or drugs involved. Only pure heart, aspiration, the "right" moment and setting, and pure Grace (for which I am eternally grateful) which prepared me for this significant experience. Part of the methods mentioned here are actually step by step and wisely developped. The other thing which I noticed to be part of a good preparation in attracting what we call "divine grace" (with the respective supramental leaps is a genuine and strong state of uplifting aspiration, a clear intention and heart purity. (Of course, having what we call "good karma" and being in the presence of evolved people makes it even more beautiful). In none of these experiences I was not using any kind of imagination or projection. Sometimes it feels as if Grace runs after you.. or as if it is there, with a cosmic patience, waiting.. but at rare moments, when certain conditions are fulfilled, some "gates" may open.. The only "problem" remaining to work through afterwards is the matter of Manifestation, where you embody what you got.. This is quite important and I noticed that many people stop at this stage. (Read more in the Creativity chapter).

I will share now a second integrative healing experience one year later, which is also related with the archetype of Wholeness. It occurred during a New Years Eve, while I was in a 7 day silent Self revelation retreat. There are certain steps in preparation, which can help a lot, once we go through them. I wasn't expecting anything, but in the same time I was completely open for the Good.

While I was centering into my heart and aiming for accessing the space of the heart *(the spiritual heart)*, on the second day of the retreat, suddenly and unexpectedly, the whole perspective I had upon life was modified. As in one instant. All that seemed to be weakness and made no sense previously, now appeared in a wonderful way; all things settled naturally in their place.

A feeling of perfect order appeared, and together with it, there was the feeling of entering in the vast space of the heart in a state of continuity of consciousness which was new to me. The feeling was actually as if a vacuum was simply calling intensely and as if swallowing me in, right there, into the heart. Almost continuously those days there was a strong activation of the energy perceived not only at the level of Anahata chakra (the heart) but also at the level of Sahasrara (crown) and Vishudha (throat) chakra.

Identification with other people or processes became natural. I tasted for the first time the sweet pure peace of the heart, for hours in a row, actually the perception was that I actually am the heart, and the heart is that what I am (the spiritual heart). This kind of state is far more than any kind of love for another. And so deeply and completely fulfilling. My heart literally became happy and with each day a state of gratitude was amplifying.

This stabilised for those days, while everything was becoming alive inside of me and around me: forgotten capacities or energies, aspirations, deep ideals, even the colours, air, people, everything was full of Life, of something new to me and so dear. The heart was palpitating in the middle of my chest as if it was a new organ, "naked" and very sensitive, more contoured, and full of life. I then discovered with amazement that my heart was perfect, without any problems. With each passing day, my heart was becoming more and more alive, together with everything else.

Then I started to feel the need to go even deeper, there was something mysterious and hidden in my heart which was calling me and that I was longing for. I had the intuition that, in order to move further, I needed more humility. So I started to simply do karma yoga in the kitchen, and in this way, the obstacle perceived like something coating the heart, melted away quite fast.

Next day, while I was meditating with *Matangi*, another great cosmic power aspect of the divine Mother, something happened. I became an immense solid channel of light, feeling alive with divine life within me, in each cell and in my breathing. A continuous ecstasy of alive light, extremely dynamic within me was pouring through all my being, even through the eyes. Silence, love, peace, and such an intense and deep gratitude that it felt as if it was breaking me in pieces, exploding inside of me, so much Good was there.

From that day on, the meditative states went deeper. With a continuous longing and burning aspiration, I was surrendering myself more and more into my heart. There was this sweet, a bit mint like substance that was dropping inside my mouth from the palate, and in great quantities... I knew it was *soma* that ancient Indians talked about. I felt it pouring all over my body and there was the feeling of being dissolved gradually in an indescribable happiness, peace and A DEEP DEEP RELAXATION. As if I was melting myself gradually, piece by piece, even physically, into light. For a few days this manifested, together with an awakening to an inner life, very alive.

We did in the last days of the retreat a meditation on revealing of the divine self through the grace of all the authentic spiritual masters. As I was centering into my heart, right from that area, it suddenly felt like as an unstopping light eruption expanding in no time, circularly in all directions. Something unstoppable and unexpected. A state of sweet peace and ecstatic happiness came into being, even if there was nothing emotional in it; it was a state of maximum simplicity possible to conceive. Natural, normal, humble. Simultaneously, I felt I was no more separated from all that exists, no barriers or contradictions or tensions remained. I was so deeply relaxed that I was perceiving I was becoming transparent and extremely easy, like a snow flake. I was feeling like flying and dancing in happiness. Secondarily, an intense and significant energising of Anahata and Sahasrara chakras was there, a state of being that was centered, lucid and clear. It was that state of bliss, being drunk with so much happiness and simplicity that prevailed. This sweet, simple, home feeling was what I was always searching for. Afterwards, for a few months I felt free, pure and quiet.

Chapter 16

Exploring the Major Archetypes: Soul's Journey towards Supramental Intelligence

There are many archetypes of the supramental: Love, Beauty, Justice, Abundance, Wholeness, Goodness, Power, and Truth are some of the major ones. In our journey of transformation beyond happiness level 3, we have to explore each of the major archetypes with inner fundamental creativity. The primary objective is to move beyond mental and emotional intelligence via brain circuits neither of which brings us unconditional happiness.

Each such creative exploration will give us upon fruition the ability to embody that archetype in tangled hierarchical relationships that not only will help us balance the negative in our life but also embody the archetype of that emotion in our character, as part of our soul. We cannot not act according to what the archetype demands from us in our relationship with people.

We must discover the living truth of all spiritual themes of life - Beauty, Justice, Abundance, Wholeness, and other time-honored values - then supramental intelligence, albeit at the soul level.

The Good-Evil Dichotomy of the Collective Unconscious: Morality and Ethics

The effort of our ancestors of the vital mind era on making representations of the Platonic archetypes in general gave us the Jungian archetypes of the collective unconscious, often split in dichotomies. In this way, via the collective unconscious, we also experience dichotomy in many archetypal areas of our life and not understanding how to manage these dichotomies creates inner conflict.

A major such dichotomy is the good-evil dichotomy: We have both a 'dark side' as well as a 'light side' to our personality. This is why seemingly 'good' people sometimes do 'bad' things.

However, just as Amit did with Love, using opposites to create new possibilities of the unconscious to precipitate conscious choice, similarly the dichotomy of good and evil can be used to propel us to a quantum leap to goodness that transcends good and evil.

Religions introduce the concept of morality as the solution of the good-evil dichotomy: "Be good because it is the moral thing to do." Of course, given the Jungian split in the collective unconscious and the negative emotional brain circuits, we cannot be good just by wishing it. We have to study the archetype of Goodness creatively and directly discover the truth of ethics. In this way, via creativity we can override built-in software of negative emotions that the collective unconscious represents.

If our educational system encourages you to check out ethics via your own creativity (it will when education changes from information to transformation), even going through the preparation stage of creativity in search of ethics, you will be a better human being. For it is a fact, that when eventually you take a quantum leap to the truth of ethics, the goodness circuit of positive emotion that you build in your brain will be quite adequate to overrule your evolutionarily inherited negativity, evil, although it may take a while to embody (manifest) your insight.

Other Archetypal Dichotomies

Good-evil is not the only dichotomy that causes trouble and division among human beings. Here is another archetype for which we experience archetypal dichotomy via the collective unconscious: the true-false dichotomy. In Platonic terms, truth is absolute, false is simply ignorance of truth. Because of the true-false dichotomy of our collective unconscious, we tend to give "false" a lot more importance than it deserves. The news media today, for example, sometimes become obsessed to maintain balance between true and false news instead of just emphasising the truth.

The brain mechanism of the building of ego-persona, reconstructive memory, builds in inauthenticity in some of the persona masks that we wear further aided by our negative emotional instincts.

Another dichotomy of the collective unconscious is the one between beauty and ugly that may have a lot to contribute to racism. White is beauty, black is ugly, according to the images of our collective unconscious. The archetype of Beauty in the Platonic sense is of course colour blind.

The social psychologist Jennifer Eberhardt has found empirical evidence for the idea above. In her experiment, she exposed people to faces subliminally—a set of black faces and a set of white faces. She then showed the subjects a blurry image of an object, which she progressively made clearer and clearer. Some of the objects were crime related like guns and knives; others were neutral like umbrellas and cameras. She found a clear bias in people: looking at black faces subliminally for a few milli-seconds prompts people to pick out guns and knives a lot sooner, reduces their recognition time significantly.

To arrive at Wholeness, we need to integrate all these dichotomies as well. Integrating the archetypal dichotomies consists eventually of exploring all the different major archetypes and bringing them down to manifestation.

Is integrating these dichotomies worth it?" The great Swami Vivekananda used to boast about his guru Ramakrishna, "My guru has the most beautiful eyes." His challengers would say, "You are biased. His eyes are just like ordinary eyes." And Vivekananda would smirk, "Where we see ugly and beauty, my guru only sees beauty. That's why he has the most beautiful eyes that do not discern such dichotomies."

Indeed, Ramakrishna treated everyone the same, rich and poor, untouchables and high caste, prostitutes and Brahmins. Isn't that ability worth having?

Awakening the Supramental

Centering into the heart is not just focusing. It is not just projecting your attention into your heart, or thinking about your heart, but being there in your heart when the experience arises. Everything that happens you will perceive it in the heart, as you are already there. For example, if you hear a noise, you feel it in your heart, not in your head. Try first, feeling it in your head, as animals do when they hear. Then, gradually bring the heart into the operational theatre.

Heart centering roots us in the present moment. As we go deeper and deeper into our heart, we go deeper and deeper into the heart of time, which is the present moment. For it, experience your awareness in the heart, and enjoy being there, more and more centered. Be connected with your body. This will calm down your mind, as the body cannot be in the past or future. You can do this by just observing your breath, as a perfectly detached witness. As you center deeper into your heart, you will feel more and more present, more and more being you, and more and more into here and now. In the same way, using this technique with a correlated partner, you can learn to CENTRE in the same time in another being's heart.

Being Present in Two Hearts at Once

In this technique we focus on our own body and another's body. We are not relating to someone else with thinking, as mental ego or mind, but with *vital energy, with the self of the heart*. We put the vital essences together. This correlates us and the other. We need to focus simultaneously into our heart, and into someone else's heart (spiritual heart). We put our awareness equally into ourselves and into the other. This is best done with someone who is very close to us. We can do it with anyone, and with everything alive (animals, plants), because in everything alive there is the potentiality of One consciousness.

Choose another person, ideally one that is very dear to you. You need to be FULLY present into yourself, and FULLY present into the other as best as you can. At the level of the quantum unconscious, this is completely possible; it will happen. You need to forget everything you know (and all judgements) about your body and the other's body as well. You can keep your eyes open or closed. However, the exercise is easier with the eyes closed. You can do it with someone who is next to you, or someone far away, or with several people at once. You need to be completely non-judgemental, simply observing, experiencing pure awareness. The sign that we are doing it right is a state of profound relaxation, profound peace. Then, just maintain the process. Do not do anything the way you are used to do. Just stay there. Normally, even several seconds are enough to trigger a very powerful experience.

The ego level is low energy. Higher energy takes us to supramental level. We need a powerful energy to get there.

Swami Adinathananda, Kashmir Shivaism teacher, described this process beautifully.

First of all, you need to centre into your heart and even forget everything you know about your body. Then project into the other's heart. Through this empathy, your hearts become perfectly tuned at the level of the essence. Feel the awakening of the supramental, and the perception limits vanishing. This is the key element of the technique. Once you return to your normal state, repeat the technique over and over.

This technique is wonderful for purifying and transforming ANY relationship even more than forgiveness and reconciliation. We re-settle this relationship as a spiritual one. You will feel free of all the sick relationships that are draining your energy. This is a complete way to overcome all problems that can appear in any relationship.

The technique is wonderful for a couple. All misunderstandings, all ego conflicts will be transformed into an ideal state of that couple when the quantum leap occurs. It can also be done with a liberated master who passed away; it is enough to have a photo of the master. You are connecting to the liberated master's nonlocal memory.

The Awakening of Supramental Intelligence at the Soul Level (Buddhi)

As our archetypal accomplishments accumulate, there begins shift of the ego-identity to a more balanced relationship of the ego with the quantum self. This shift is an important part of the awakening of supramental intelligence at the soul level, called *buddhi* in Sanskrit. Etymologically, intelligence comes from the root word intelligo which means "to select among." Appropriate, isn't it? Indeed, with the awakening of *buddhi*, we can do no wrong in our selection. This is why it is also called *discriminative intelligence*.

The buddhi level of being brings a welcome freedom from compulsive self-preoccupation and preoccupation with the material world which promotes transactional relationships, you may sometimes feel this freedom when you sing in the shower or walk in the woods, maybe even in some relationships like mother child or of romance. Can you imagine feeling that kind of freedom during what you call chores, what you call boredom, or even what you call suffering? It is like dancing through life. "Will you, won't you, will you, won't you, won't you join the dance?" This exuberant invitation from Lewis Carroll is always open to all of us, but we thrive in such dancing only when supramental intelligence awakens. Read what the great Sufi mystic/poet Rumi has to say on archetypes:

> *[Archetypal] Journeys bring power and love*
> *back into you. If you can't go somewhere,*
> *move in the passageways of the [quantum] self.*
> *They are like shafts of light,*
> *always changing, and you change*
> *when you explore them.*

Chapter 17

Integrating the Head and the Heart

For supramental intelligence to fully awaken even though compromised, even though it is only at the soul level of higher mind and higher vital, we must fully integrate mind and the vital - head and the heart. The main problem here is that the thinking self of the brain is a strong ego. Evolutionarily speaking we are in the stage of the rational mind. Under the aegis of scientific materialism and the advent of information technology, even many women in America now feel offended if they are called emotional. In contrast, because of the male-female difference, at least one of the two selves in the body is weak; for the male, it is the heart self that is weak, for the female it is the navel.

What loses out is our capacity to feel love in the body. Think about it! How can you truly love another without loving yourself ? And vice versa. How can you love yourself without knowing that love is an expansion of consciousness, not a contraction as in narcissism?

Only when we integrate the navel and the heart, we develop the unified experience of the self in the body, a self centered on the experience of feeling. And this what is called the *awakening* of the *heart* in the spiritual traditions.

As men discover their heart chakra by direct experience even in non-romantic relationships, they are surprised to find that they don't really have to be the "iron men" they try to be. Similarly, when women discover their navel chakra and self-worth, they find they don't have to join the lonely- hearts club if they don't have some man to love.

In this way, emotional intelligence which begins with the making of positive emotional brain circuits becomes mature with the integration of male-female individual chakra-identity.

Some time ago I (Amit) saw a play named Cloud Nine. One of its episodes is about a lonely older woman who never masturbated. In the last quite touching scene, this woman learns to do "it" which is depicted on the stage as the woman dancing with herself and waking up to self- love and emotional intelligence.

Do Men and Women Think Differently?

We have already spoken of integrating the feeling aspects of male-female difference, the body selves. How about thinking? The sociologist Carol Gilligan, in a book *In a Different Voice* written at the height of the feminist movement in the seventies proposed a model of male-female difference on the basis of how they think, not how they feel. This work was different from the first wave of feminism at the time in that it did not stop with suggesting that women did not think hierarchically whereas men do.

From a spiritual/ethical point of view, nonhierarchical thinking is better than hierarchical thinking. You are listening to the quantum self, tangled hierarchy, right? Not quite so fast, said Gilligan correctly. We, even the females among us need to go through transformational stages before we are able to give up the habit of imposing simple hierarchy of the ego/persona in our actions.

What does nonhierarchical thinking mean? Thinking with love, thinking with giving relationship considerations the priority. Yes, the female among us have some natural ability in doing that because their heart is more open than the male; biology and society does that. Does that make female thinking better? Depends. Don't forget the same biological and social tendencies give the female a weak navel identity, less self-respect which always compromises the other love. In this way, there will be contradiction in the female attempt of behaving non-hierarchically. It will be a mistake to think that all women or even a majority of women of the dominating and colonising West were against domination or women in American deep South have always opposed the Ku Klux Klan. It seems better to conclude with another feminist Barbara Ehrenreich that "a uterus is not substitute for a conscience," and let go at that.

This is why it is optimal first to integrate the navel and the heart, develop a clear self of the body that we call *our heart*. If we do that, then male and female thinking become harmonised after some practice.

Conscience, Morality, Viveka, and All That

Every society has a concept of morality or conscience for which the Sanskrit word is *viveka*. It is an ability to distinguish between good and evil or do the right thing, to be fair, to love. In other words there is no unique definition except that we can discriminate between good and evil or just and unjust, there is an innate ability.

The spiritual metaphysics of blanket oneness supports this discriminating ability; it gave rise to the concept of morality. Today, the concept of *morality* no longer is even applied to guide people's action now that scientific materialism has challenged that idea.

In the West especially there has been so much effort towards formulating a science of ethics and some great philosophers have been associated with that - Spinoza and Kant, just to name two. Kant had the idea of categorical imperative: it is imperative for humans to act morally, ethically.

Religions use fear to institute morality in society: it is sin to act unethically. And you have to pay for it after death. In Christianity you are sent to hell; in the East you are reincarnated as an animal, and you stay that way at least until you pay your karmic debt to the person you wronged.

Ethics is legit in the quantum worldview, nonlocality - oneness implies that, but nonlocality is not imperative because unity consciousness is not imperative; I don't have to become correlated with you. As for punishment for unethical behaviour, the quantum view is that people are already being punished for their dalliance; they are not able to access their potentialities.

When we make effort to have nonlocal and tangled hierarchical relationship with others, we begin to develop a conscience or the power of discrimination between good and evil, fair and unfair, beauty and ugly, truth and false. These dichotomies are the product of our anthropological history, the incomplete archetypal representation in our collective unconscious. When these dichotomies are transformed, integrated and transcended, then we have the ability to discriminate correctly.

Without integrating the dichotomies, without integrating the navel and the heart modern men try to do it with lawfulness and justice; in other words employing incomplete concepts of the archetypes of truth and justice no matter where they get them from, perhaps mostly from religion and a bit from parents and teachers.

Women, without the integration of feelings in the body try to do it with incomplete notion of goodness and love. I referred to Gilligan's work above; she, correctly sees the male-female difference of thinking this way.

In quantum spirituality, we first integrate the two selves of the body, so that our feelings speak unambiguously from one strong voice - the heart. Goodness and Love have both been attended to; for these two archetypes the representation in terms of feelings is the important one. For the archetypes of Truth and Justice on the other hand, it is the brain's thinking self which we have to engage. To integrate heart and the head is also to integrate all four archetypes to enable us to find appropriate action. Then supramental intelligence.

Amit's Awakening of the Heart

I reported my *anima* dream earlier. In the dream, this young woman, when she parted, said "I am going to London," but she promised to return. In 1998, I fell in love and had my third marriage with a delightful woman twenty years younger than me; I immediately recognised this as the return of anima of my life and in the next five years I enjoyed our relationship but did nothing to integrate my anima within myself.

When the romantic juice invariably ran out as it always does, I had to pay attention which I did as reported in chapter 14; and eventually it all ended with my breakthrough to an insight about unconditional love. And then the question of vital creativity came back to me. How do I feel the love for my partner in the heart independent of the brain?

In other words, How do I make the body selves - navel and heart - conscious? I began practicing integrating the navel and the heart chakra energies as one tangled hierarchy. Traditional Chinese medicine also propounds the idea that at the vital level, the vital components of organs influence one another, a fact supported by the data that paying attention to the meridians in between helps the health of the heart organs.

Many years ago, under a teacher's direction I had read a book by a Christian mystic which I did not understand much at all except that its name, *Practicing the Presence of God* stuck out. Those words came back to me and inspired me to start a practice that I aptly named practicing the presence of love. It consisted of meditating on love at the heart. I did it in the same spirit as I do *japa*, silently repeating a *mantra*: keep the love-in-the-heart awareness whenever I remembered. After a while, it becomes stabilized; whenever I checked, the heart had love in it, it felt expanded.

Then one day, the miracle happened. Many years ago, I had that Samadhi experience culminating a japa meditation for seven long days, you remember (see chapter 2). Subsequent to that experience, I remained in a state for two days when loving another was unconditional and compulsory. That state now came back. Not with so much intensity and fanfare this time, mind you.

I was talking with a woman who clearly was behaving like an adversary; there was much antagonism between us. All of a sudden my heart sent a signal, and whatever antagonism I was feeling just stopped. I could only love the woman in spite of all that antagonism. My heart was open. And it spoke its own voice! After a forty-year absence, unconditional and inclusive love had returned to me.

The night I wrote the above, I couldn't sleep; something was bothering me. It was that "aha-surprise" thing that should come with a quantum leap. I never had that in my exploration of the archetype of Love; if there were surprise, they were little bangs, not the expected big one.

Then it dawned on me, an Aha moment. That experience in 1976 when I felt love and nothing but love for everyone I interacted with, was my big Aha moment of fundamental creativity and the insight was for the archetype of Wholeness. I was so unprepared that not only did I not realise it at the time, but also I had been carrying out the manifestation stage of that creative realisation ever since without knowing it.

Was Wholeness even on my plate in 1976 and love too? Very much so. In chapter 2, I told you about the crystallisation experience when I knew that my chosen archetype for this life is Wholeness. A year later, I married (my second) a white American woman who said to me, "I love you but I am not in love with you. I see there is something in you which is very pure and that attracts me very much. So I will marry you." So indeed: both Wholeness and Love were on my plate of exploration.

Going back a little bit. Why was it important to integrate my male and the unconscious female within me before I could love another unconditionally, really open my heart? It's that self-respect thing. If I cannot love and respect my own heart, how can I love and respect another's? If I cannot love and respect my own head, how can I love and respect another's?

A special note. Here are the specific instructions for the meditation of practicing the presence of love. Simply bring your energy to your heart chakra by visualising somebody you love or any of the other ways you have learned to make the heart come alive. Hold the energy for a few minutes. And then as you go through your day, periodically check if energy is still there at the heart. If it is there, fine; if not, bring back the energy. After a while, the energy in the heart will become internalised: whenever you look, you will find energy in your heart.

More Exercises

In order to remain for longer time in a supramental state you can use an "anchor" for your attention at that level. One very strong such "anchor" is the focusing into the present moment. The present moment is one of the most effective ways to enter and maintain yourself into the supramental level since it is only in the present moment the inferior mind (*manas* in Sanskrit) will be blocked.

You are focusing the mind upon the present moment and gradually the mental agitation start to diminish and disappear. The mind is an instrument, a vehicle for your consciousness. The present moment where only consciousness "lives" and no vehicles can go there. Follow the silence and do not be concerned where the noise is left on the way.

Another easy anchoring of the attention is to focus upon a brand-new perceptive with act-taking "the road less traveled" or not travelled at all-since according to one of the fundamental universal principles any such act happens with present-centeredness. Try to be aware whenever you have an act of perception of something new is in the offing and notice the effects.

Chapter 18

Quantum Enlightenment

In chapter 2, I (Amit) described my creative breakthrough to an insight of inclusive love - Wholeness. I did no conceptual preparation to speak of; if there were any, I did not premeditate on it. I did not know what unconscious processing or do-be-do-be-do is about. I just did a seven- days *japa* meditation with as much sincerity as I could master. I was lucky. Call it beginner's mind, God's Grace, Whatever.

How does one go systematically in exploring the archetype of Wholeness? Some integration of the three major dichotomies of the human condition is a major step of the preparation stage of the creative process for the exploration of Wholeness. Initially you employ situational creativity. Then you explore the archetype itself in its suchness. The creative process here is that of *fundamental creativity*.

To recap, the basic process is do-be-do-be-do. The purpose of "do" is to create new ideas of imagination - divergent thinking

- as seeds for expansion into full- blown possibility pools via the "be" phase of unconscious processing for consciousness to choose from. Insightful ideas may come, integrative ideas. Look for the surprise element and the element of conviction- I know. Being human, initially you are going to make mistakes in gauging these insightful ideas for their surprise - wishful thinking. Don't be dismayed. Failures are the pillars of success. Conviction will be lacking if that is the case and will bring you back to more do-be-do-be-do. Truth values cannot be simulated except for psychopaths.

If you are ill with one of those diseases that are chronic conditions - cancer, heart disease, clinical depression- you should approach the healing path, exploration of Wholeness, with the help of a medical professional. Since our interest is more in healing the mental/emotional, let's discuss depression as an example. You may wonder if this is appropriate since we are discussing positive mental health. Relax! It is very appropriate if it fits the bill. Many mystics talk about the "dark night of the soul." Make no mistake, it is not about one night! They are talking about depression of a specific kind. Since you are looking for Wholeness, depression which is an intensely felt lack of Wholeness, is often the result. You have found the problem: what is the worth of human life if we are not whole?

How does a therapist help? All mental health practitioners are interested in their own Wholeness; that is why they have chosen their profession. So a trusted therapist (not a psychiatrist, those guys are believers in allopathic medicine to balance neurochemicals in your brain; they think all depression is caused by neurochemical imbalance) can provide additional help towards providing fodder for unconscious processing. It is like allowing a double slit arrangement for the unconscious processing of your thoughts.

And if your therapist is what you call an intimate relationship, you two can even disagree setting up a conflicted dynamic as illustrated by Picasso's Minoteur (fig. 15). This thesis and antithesis sets up brand new possibilities for consciousness to choose from in the part of the unconscious that we call *quantum unconscious and traditions call the abode of God.*

Then it comes, THE QUANTUM LEAP, THE CREATIVE INSIGHT. Don't worry, when the real Mccoy arrives, you will know. Both surprise and conviction would be unmistakable!

Jiddu Krishnamurthy is right when he said, *Truth is a pathless land* except that no path does not imply that a *guru* is not useful. The role of the *guru* is not to set the path, but to act as a collaborator in a mutually supportive exploration and provide a mirror and a source of inspiration.

How do you manifest an archetype so discovered in fundamental creativity? You live the discovered truth about the archetype in your relationships. Your relationships become tangled hierarchical incorporating the new discovered meaning.

What does this really mean? It means, at this stage the manifestation consists of what spiritual traditions call *surrendering your will to God's will.* In the scientific language, we live on our intuition as what Carl Jung called *the intuitive personality type.* The brain will make memory of your acting out, but not of your new character trait. That trait will be permanently with you in potentiality even in your subsequent incarnations.

Mythologically speaking, the hero discovers the Truth of an archetype, and returns to teach it. As he or she teaches, and as his/her new character manifests, his/ her relationship to people changes from simple to tangled hierarchy; in this way, the hero is said to become a saviour.

We speak of transformation much in psychology as well as spiritual traditions. What is transformation? If you say, the ability to live in the quantum self, basically that answer is correct. Your centre of gravity has shifted towards the quantum self. How does another person know it? Anyone can claim to live in the quantum self. Another person, especially your intimate relationships can know via your ability to establish empathic and tangled hierarchical relationship with them. First in matters of that one archetype that you embodied in your character, and then as you explore and embody more archetypes, and eventually the archetype of Wholeness, this ability to engage tangled hierarchy in your relationships with the world becomes your way of living. Then you can be said to be fully transformed. You have all the supramental intelligence the soul level is capable of.

More on the Manifestation Stage

To emphasise once again, in the manifestation stage of an archetypal insight, you don't concentrate on creating a brain circuit which is ephemeral; instead, you concentrate on changing your character. You become whole in your dealings with people; in other words you cultivate that tangled hierarchy in your relationship as you embody the archetype. The brain will make memory of your acting out and these memories are useful in situations where your intuition is not forthcoming. Your new character trait which is part of your nonlocal memory will be the guiding light of your life.

In quantum psychology we call this "soul-level existence happiness of level 5". You more or less live in continuous flow with the quantum self in your waking hours.

Long term meditators of mindfulness in a specific practice of loving kindness show evidence for this: their brain is full of gamma activity, those brain waves of forty Hertz or more frequency. This is highly significant because flow takes them to the quantum self experience whose signature is the gamma burst - an explosive creation of high frequency synchronous gamma movement in the brain. So naturally a brain scan would show the presence of high frequency gamma. And indeed, these people are creatively exploring the archetype of love; they go through the do-be-do-be-do in their meditation. Their mind is so slow the two aspects, do – awareness - is interspersed with be - no awareness. And a quantum leap occurs sometime in the process; of course that is hard to measure. But the little bangs of flow in the manifestation stage of their creative insight leaves a signature in their brain, and that is what the researchers are measuring. Read Goleman and Davidson's book, *Altered Traits*.

Increased quantum self experience with the clear signature of synchronous gamma activity is what I predict happens in people of inner creativity as they are manifesting their creative insights. I reemphasise: the experience is called *flow*. In the new science, it is an encounter between the ego and the quantum self. Ego gives form and the quantum self provides the insight and inspiration. Read my book *Quantum Creativity*.

We declare: *the realisation of the archetype of Wholeness and its subsequent embodiment, is also a form of enlightenment.* I would call it quantum enlightenment since it does involve practically ongoing happiness that comes with ongoing encounters with the quantum self. We can also call this state the *bodhisattva state*. The advantage of encouraging the cultivation of this kind of enlightenment in our current culture over the traditional enlightenment is enormous. Spiritual seekers no more have to be confused about all that talk about giving up the ego and wonder how one can live without an ego in today's world. In quantum enlightenment, you get to be in both quantum self and the ego. Isn't it like having your cake and eating it too?

Happiness and Intelligence in Living in Flow

Creative experiences of manifestation are partly a joyful encounter with the quantum self, sometimes quite prolonged- the flow state. Are you curious if it possible to live in a state of continuous flow? Have people done that?

Recap. When we manifest the creative insight in the manifestation stage, a playful encounter takes place between the ego and the quantum self--the flow experience. Every time we engage in fundamental creativity to discover new meaning in a new archetypal context, we can either further explore the new context by many investigations of situational creativity or alternatively, we can investigate a different archetype; either way we go through the same process creating more ongoing experiences of flow.

In fact, we can set up a life with a network of creative enterprises in which each enterprise picks up the slack when we are resting from another. In this way, our life becomes an ongoing flow experience. This is one way of joyful living with the ongoing touch of the quantum self. What is it like? In the words of the poet Walt Whitman:

> To me, every hour of the light and dark is a miracle
>
> Every inch of space is miracle
>
> Every square yard of the surface of the earth
>
> is spread with the same
>
> Every cubic foot of the interior swarms with the same.
>
> (Whitman, The Leaves of Grass, p. 165.)

Or heed the words of another connoisseur Rabindranath Tagore:

> I have listened
>
> And I have looked with open eyes
>
> I have poured my soul into this world
>
> Seeking the unknown within the known.
>
> And I sing out loud
>
> In amazement.

This is the sort of quantum living that is very appropriate for the transformation-oriented people of quantum worldview in the twenty-first century: living with one foot firmly on the ground - strong ego and all - and the other foot in the fluidity of the miraculous quantum self. It is time to acknowledge the contribution of people of this level - Walt Whitman, Rabindranath Tagore, Mahatma Gandhi and Dalai Lama are recent examples - to human civilization. These people satisfied their drive of Wholeness via a new mode for interacting with others. Ordinary people interact with locality and in this way become correlated; this satisfies their drive to unity, the "I" in part gives way to a greater "we" - unity whenever they connect. These people of flow use tangled hierarchy to interact with other people when serving the archetypes they discovered; in this way for them the meaning of we is an extended "I." People of level 5 use tangled hierarchy in virtually all of their relationships since they have explored most of the important archetypes to fruition. They live in the world as if *the world is their family.*

I will end this chapter with a story from the Upanishads. A young boy, his name Nachiketa, wants to know the nature of reality, the whole shebang. Who can teach it but Yama, the death God? No matter, the boy goes to Yama's abode and fasts and fasts and prays and prays. Yama gives him an audience and is satisfied with the authenticity of the boy's inquiry. Yama explains the nature of reality to Nachiketa and so pleased is he with the boy's receptivity, he grants some blessings to the boy so he can go back to the world and excel. Let the spirit of Yama's last words to Nachiketa inspire you:

> *Rise up, wake up, understand and fulfil your potentialities.*

That's what the human life is for!

Chapter 19

The Awakening of Supramental Intelligence in Suchness

"Supramental" refers to what is beyond the vital, beyond the mental realm, beyond our common intellect, beyond the soul, beyond what we are used to process, understand, and communicate.

Our intellect is always offering pictures of reality, and not the reality itself. It is like a photo camera: if the camera is shaking, then the pictures are of very poor quality, and they can be very far from reality, lacking in meaning or sense. The supramental is "archetypal experience with knowledge and feeling." If we just have the knowledge but no feeling, it is dry, it does not transform us. If we just have the experience of feeling without the mental knowledge, we do not know what it is; it is foggy to say the least, and we cannot maintain it.

The knowledge can help us to stabilise the experience in us. Knowledge + feeling in experience is the perfect combination, is the right approach to the supramental. This is what we do for what is called "soul-making".

The first time I (Valentina) heard about this was from Swami Adinathananda's Vijnana Bhairava Tantra teachings. Afterwards, plenty of quantum worldview elements added, and altogether created a remarkable integrative effect upon myself, and as well upon my relationships. A supramental experience of creative insight can be life changing; the mental-vital memory or representation and the supramental association with it is yours forever, you can recreate the memory/experience whenever you want. The inspiration guides and helps you through the process of embodiment or manifestation; that is how you change, transform, and build your soul.

Get this. Our 'mother-soul' the supramental in suchness speaks in a language we cannot directly learn. Our feelings translate it into movement of energy. Our mind speaks about it in soul-speak still in words. Only when the supramental intelligence in suchness awakens in us can we transcend this world of soul-speak. Then we can make our own archetypal symbology of them; via nonlocal correlations/associations the symbols when evoked will take us to the supramental in suchness. If we do this in a tribal collective consciousness, these symbols may become universal. This must be is how our ancestors created the collective unconscious- all those realms of angels, devas, and such.

You notice that all of the exploration agenda of quantum spirituality and the archetype of Wholeness, true mental intelligence, emotional intelligence, evolutionary ethics, and deep ecology, require occasional forays to the domain of the supramental via fundamental creativity. If we keep doing this en masse, it should be obvious that much of humanity will be capable of growing into supramental intelligence when the next step of our evolution from rational to intuitive mind gains momentum. So instead of personal liberation via the exploration of the self, we make Wholeness and evolution our priority.

This is a very profound change and its time has come. When liberation is our goal, when it is liberation or bust, we become exclusively centred on personally arriving at the quantum self identity which remains elusive. The achievement orientation itself becomes a barrier to the goal. When we centre on evolution and the archetype of Wholeness, it is not all or nothing any more, and we value the insights gained on the path. We engage in evolutionary ethics to gain insight in the archetype of goodness; we engage in creativity in science to develop insights in the archetype of truth; we engage in aesthetics and the arts and architecture to gain insights in the archetype of beauty and resolve the dichotomy of beauty and ugly; we engage in emotional intelligence practice in intimate relationship to gain insight in the archetype of love; we engage in law, news media, even politics to gain insight about the archetype of justice and power; and so forth. These insights are invaluable for integrating those archetypal dichotomies of the collective unconscious that our ancestors created.

When we stabilise the insights gained by those supramental journeys we make in how we live our lives, we are acquiring characteristics of supramental intelligence. To some, this would seem quite imperfect; our mental- vital representations of the supramental will never match the real thing, they would (correctly) point out. This is the best we can do; we are preparing the entire human race for the eventual next step in its evolution - the omega point, the capacity to make physical representations of the supramental. We don't entirely give up our journey towards liberation, but we put that on the back-burner useful only for those few who get a burnout.

The supramental in suchness is engaging with archetypal intuition transcending the mind-brain and heart and navel in a process of superior understanding of the archetype with both feeling and meaning integrated and transcended. How do we do this?

Behold! The supramental is not foreign to us. All the "Aha!" moments, revelations, discoveries, getting a different perspective, moments when we are not so predictable, when we simply follow our heart defying common sense, when we do exactly what we feel to do that is non-rational (but not irrational).

The access to supramental in suchness is very direct, discontinuous in time. The challenge is to maintain the capacity, to stay present, to continue the practice, so the moments of revelation do not miss us, become more frequent, and last longer and longer. The approach is completely non-judgmental. It is simply by observing with attention and intention, experiencing, pure awareness.

Discipline comes from the word *disciple*. It implies the ability to be your own disciple, to follow you heart all the time, to be able to perceive the hidden messages that are beyond your mind, and follow them. If you have states of *Samadhi* only in meditation, it becomes something that you call *sacred* - apart from the mundane part of your life. It means you are not really transformed. You need to integrate the supramental and samadhi in your entire life. You discover expanded consciousness in you, in all situations of your life. Then you create a unity in your life. This is the principle of double integration: integrate your life into spirituality, and spirituality into your life.

Joining the Rest of the Universe

Back to the beginning. Often we are confronted with life situations and dilemmas that we cannot solve from the mental perspective for the simple reason that we have the impression we need more data. At a closer look we realise that lost in the labyrinth of the mind, we find it very difficult to make a decision, not because we do not have the information but because there are so many viewpoints upon the same information.

Yet, the outcome is always clear in the end and sometimes we say: *I should have said that, or I should have done this…* And there are some blessed moments in life when we feel great, we feel in high spirits and we see things with a kind of eagle eye view, accurately getting all the details and at the same time having an extraordinarily broad perspective that allows us to take the right decision in no time.

From that perspective everything appears very clear, nothing is foggy or too complex anymore. The question that often arises is: *How can one regularly access this eagle-eye view?*

The answer is in a special state of consciousness that is only accessible after quite some radical transformations. This is the supramental state that Sri Aurobindo discovered but could not embody because it cannot be embodied in the physical body that we have. In this supramental state, the mental structure, including those of the higher mind or soul, is transcended, the discursive mind (the producer of all the dualistic thoughts) is silenced because we no longer feed it with our attention. For many, this supramental state might appear very difficult to obtain but with little effort we can easily understand (at least intellectually) the reality of this state that is just one blink, one quantum leap away from our soul level of being.

This supramental state is a state which is characterised by first, the awareness, and second, the preparatory exploration (soul-building), and third, the penetration of what is called vital and mental sheaths (including what we call soul). Its embodiment requires the building of an energetic structure beyond the mental and vital sheaths that includes higher mind (and higher vital) of the soul. This is the energetic structure of your being responsible for integrating you with the universe, making the subtle connections that translate the individuality - body, mind, soul - into universality in its right time and place. Everyone has this energetic structure in waiting, in potentiality; however, very few have it awakened to the level of conscious awareness; for most people it is just a potentiality.

Many years ago, when I (Amit) had a beginner's mind, I saw a dream. In the dream there was a radiant being and I was looking at him with indescribable joy. I could not but look at him; the joy was so enticing, I looked at him the whole time. When I woke up in the morning I shared my dream with my teacher at the time; the teacher's eyes became large and he said, "Amit don't you know what the dream means? You were looking at yourself at a future time."

Sri Aurobindo did many years of exploration towards this supramental state and eventually did awaken to it. But from the analysis of his later life, the scientific conclusion has to be that he was not able to stabilize these energy structures required. The conclusion is what I have been saying all along. It is impossible to make direct representations of the supramental archetype in the earthly physical body of ordinary matter.

The participation of our life in the universal life in absence of the penetration into this supramental level of a different kind of physical existence is very limited at the level of positive mental health, or even the soul or the higher mind though these levels are beyond the level of survival to be sure. Even from the exalted perspective of positive mental health or the soul, our access to the universal life is governed by synchronicity. It is likely that upon awakening to the awareness of the supramental structure, we become aware of the permanent interaction that takes place between the individuality and the totality, making everything coherent and synchronised. In spiritual traditions, this is described as a rebirth in a universal physical body while this earthly physical body remains an option. Is this scientific? With the discovery that 25% of the matter of the universe is a more "subtle" dark matter, gives us hope that a science of such a universal physical body is not very far off our horizon.

One simple characteristic of this trans mental-vital energetic level of our being is that it does not depend on any particular aspect of life, it is that universal part of our being that is specifically designed for all of us. This supramental structure is concealed to our normal rational level of awareness; it is beyond our cognitive ability because our awareness is completely locked into details of our personal melodrama, reducing all that is general and universal to something that is particular. For example, when you stay here in this room, you stay here in this particular room. Now, what is particular about this room? Is it the address? Is it the colour of the walls or the floor? Or is it the particular memories that we have attached to it? In reality it's just a mental box that you have created and associated with all these particular attributes. In reality, it's just a room like any other but we see it not as just a room, we see it as being this particular room only. Its universality is hidden behind the particular details attached to it by our ordinary rational mind, *manas*.

For people of rational mind, this is what they usually call *reality* and therefore they are locked into this particular room. Also because the senses are "shouting" all these details to them that they unconsciously associate themselves and with this particular room, they create this reality as the reality. Thus the supramental level, from where the whole concept of mental being here was born, is covered up by all the specific details and as a result we can't perceive it at all or perceive it at best as a set of physical laws that we cannot penetrate. This is of course essential for consciousness to create life and mind and evolution on a planet.

Even if concealed by the details of reality, it is possible for anyone to conceptualise this supramental state right now thanks to the power of quantum science, and then resolve to penetrate the mental and vital and gain momentary access to the supramental with further transformative efforts. Even while you are reading these lines you are formulating your ideas and fundamental experiences at the supramental level in the shape of some intuitions and intentions, but they get immediately "swallowed" at the mental level where you just assign them to the particular personality you have – you give them the personal flavour of your thoughts until everything becomes an on-going saga of the very detailed personality that cannot be distinguished from its basic elements.

It is exactly like for example, when you look at a pointillist painting when you can't see the individual dots of colours because the colours are contained already in the images that create the whole painting. Therefore, you can't see only the red dot for example, if you are looking at the painting as a whole. Analogically speaking, this is how the supramental state is concealed in the normal daily states we have.

There are some elements related to the mental work that we usually ignore (and we pay a great price for this ignorance): the associative power of the inferior ordinary mind (manas) that combines the past experiences with the present perceptions to create a predictable future through projections. From this perspective we can say that the inferior mental structure is working with the domains of the past and future. In the absence of these two dimensions of time (past and future) the inferior mind is blocked because there is nothing to associate the perceptions from the present moment with. With this observation, you can easily understand why the present moment can be – when attentively observed – a genuine gate to the supramental state. When the inferior mind stops, the supramental state shines forth.

Another analogy that is often used in the spiritual tradition is the surface of a lake. When the water is disturbed by waves created by exterior factors or by inner movements of the water, then you can see the reflections of the light and of the sky on the water but they will only show the surface of the water with millions of sparks of shattered images reflected on it. When the water is very still, then we cannot see its surface anymore because we see only the bottom of the lake. The reflective surface apparently disappears disclosing what was concealed by the chaotic reflection on the agitated surface: the lake-bed that supports the lake itself. Analogically, the supramental is the lake-bed that is supporting all the mental/emotional activities and it is concealed by the result of these activities. Its potentiality is actualised as soon as these activities are stopped. The soul level is the preparation for achieving the calm surface of the lake water.

There are many methods to silence the mind and they are quite easy to practice "the difficulty is to make the sacrifice of all the meaningless but apparently useful details that we keep in the inferior mind, these will vanish once the mind is still." For most people, meditation and mental training fails the moment they have to decide to give up the content of the inferior mind; for many the inferior mind looks like the house of an old lady, filled with all the old stuff she cannot throw away because of their *emotional value.*

It is said that when Einstein was preparing to leave Hitler's Germany for America, his wife, in charge of packing the household goods, could not decide what to leave behind. Einstein joked, "You are attached to the furniture." It was no kidding.

This gives us another method for accessing a glimpse at the supramental state apart from the gradualist approach of developing a soul level of existence and living first: the focus of the attention upon the present moment. Mystics such as Jiddu Krishnamurthy and Ekhart Tolle advocate it. The inferior mind exists only in the context of using the past and future as a basis of its associations. When focusing only upon the present moment, the inferior mind is still, frozen in the golden moment of now. At that moment the supramental state can shine forth.

Even so, it is impossible to live in the supramental state as a homeostasis while in our gross earthly physical body; momentarily getting out of the sheaths of the vital and mental koshas is not enough, we need new memory-making ability. About a subtler physical body capable of such memory-making, we can only speculate.

For tired souls who want liberation from birth-death-rebirth cycle, this is the time to explore the Self archetype. After the insight called *self-realisation*, the adept manifests the selfless living and since quantum self provides no homeostasis, there is only one place to live: in the unconscious but in the unity consciousness, the unconscious realm of previously un-manifest potentialities. This is what spiritual traditions call

God-realisation. In India, this state is called *Nirvikalpa Samadhi* or *Turiya*. This is discussed further in my book *Quantum Creativity.*

Even while developing the soul level, training this focus upon the present moment even just for a few moments a day, will start to awaken the intention for supramental intelligence in suchness, for a supramental being in manifestation. The wisdom traditions assure us that such being is possible; science tells us we cannot have such manifestation in this physical body.

A Course in Miracles hints at a science of eternity. Are there people who live in manifest eternity? As scientists, as quantum activists, as partially awakened souls, we shall go on investigating.

What if?...

We will end this chapter with a highly speculative idea. We do not know much yet about the kundalini awakening of the seventh crown chakra. What we do know is that the chakra is connected to the function of the posterior superior parietal lobe (PSPL)—producing body image and identification with the physical body. Neuroscientific evidence is already suggesting that when people have out-of-the-body experience, the PSPL activity is much reduced.

We have also mentioned the assertion in spiritual literature about a rebirth in sambhogakaya body after death when one qualifies for it. This sambhogakaya body may be made of dark matter.

The big question is what qualifies a person for the privilege of a sambhogakaya body? It may very well be the experience of the Wholeness archetype in suchness not only in the mental plane but also in the vital plane. The latter consists of the kundalini awakening of the crown chakra.

If one is reborn in a sambhogakaya body, it comes with the capacity of making direct representation of archetypes. In subsequent incarnations in earth matter, this sambhogakaya body would be available nonlocally, via the mediation of consciousness, to make direct memories of supramental experiences without resorting to mind or the vital. In his way, such an earthly being would also gain some cosmic connection.

Chapter 20

Can One Experience The Archetypes Without Separateness?

There are talks in the spiritual literature of India about *Savikalpa Samadhi* (*Samadhi* with separateness) and *Nirvikalpa Samadhi* (*Samadhi* without separateness), both refer to the self archetype. *Savikalpa Samadhi* is the experience of self realisation. It is reached by the creative process of fundamental creativity like any other archetype. That being the case, the creative moment of 'aha' for any archetype can be called a *savikalpa* realisation of the archetype.

The *Nirvikalpa* state of *Samadhi* is reached in the manifestation stage of the creative process for the self-archetype. If our analogy is correct, and why should it not be? Then there should be a reachable *Nirvikalpa* states for each archetype.

In this book, we have talked about individual bodies that we have, that we develop: the physical body, the vital body, the mental body, and the higher mind-higher vital that we call *the soul* that represents our archetypal experiences approximately. We can even call our unity consciousness, of which the *quantum self experience* is the doorway, as a fifth body. In the Upanishads, these bodies are called *kosha*, for which the English word is sheath. You can find these ideas and their scientific explanation in the upcoming book *See the World* as a *Five Layered Cake.*

The fifth sheath is called *Anandamaya* kosha because it has no structural or even functional boundaries, only unlimited joy called *Turiyananda*; the realization of the Self archetype leads to the realization that the self is a no-self, the (quantum) self is the doorway to unity, doorway to penetrate all koshas including the *Vigyanamaya kosha* (the fourth kosha corresponding to the supramental) into the *Anandamaya kosha*. The price for the entry is to give up all attachments, all desires. Only then whenever we process in the unconscious, we are the quantum unconscious of previously unmanifest possibilities over which God presides. So, we can fall into God, *Anandamaya kosha*, in the *Nirvikalpa* state of *Turiya*.

Can we not think of *Anandamaya* kosha as the abode of the Self archetype whose true nature is God? By the same token, can we not expect that there would be a *Nirvikalpa* experience for each of the archetypes and that a land in the *Vigyanamaya* world can be assigned for such a location (*loka* in Sanskrit)?

What would it be like to experience such an archetypal land in *Nirvikalpa*? You can only describe what you experience after you wake up from your visit of your archetypal land. And using what? The mental representations of the collective unconscious. In this way, we get vivid descriptions of the archetypal land in the spiritual literature of India; a recent example is Ramakrishna's experiences of the goddess Kali. Another example is that of Mohammad who spoke of experiences with the archangel Gabriel. Another example is Carmelite nuns who speak of experiences with Jesus.

If you have not heard of Kali, the great Nelson Mandela made her famous when he visited India some years ago. When he was asked what city of India he enjoyed most, to everyone's surprise he said, Calcutta (now Kolkata). When asked to explain he said, because *that's the only city where a female black goddess* (yes, that is how Kali is depicted) *tramples over a white male god (Shiva).*

Another million-dollar question. What would be the archetypal image of the Wholeness archetype? Is there any reference to the archetype of wholeness in the reports about great sages who visit this archetype?

Surprisingly there is, a lot of reference to such visits and the people who have done it. The most famous of these people is the legendary rishi *Narada* who regularly visited Goloka where the Wholeness archetype - *MahaVishnu* - resides. Not coincidentally, another name of *Mahavishnu* is Narayana that literally translates as path (yana) of nara (human being). Narayana - the archetype of Wholeness - is the path to spirituality for the ordinary human who stays in the ego.

Ok, is there any more well-known image? In India, there is also a much misunderstood concept of the *avatara*, popularly understood as "God incarnate or son of God." Truly, this does not make any scientific sense if you tend to see God as the agent of downward causation or Brahman with qualification or quantum consciousness. No, here the source of the *avatara* has to be MahaVishnu; indeed, the avataras of Indian mythology are called incarnations of *MahaVishnu*.

Usually, *MahaVishnu* would not take incarnate form with all of its wholeness, but only as a part *avatara* which will be depicted as one of the lesser archetype such as Justice (*Rama*). The only exception is *Krishna*. *Krishna* is called *purnaavatara*, the *avatara* of Wholeness itself. The Sanskrit word *purna* means Wholeness.

The Indian myths go deep in significance. The first one goes like this. *Dharma* or *Tao* is in deep trouble on earth.

The gods (the representations of archetypes in our collective unconscious) are debating whether to send Wholeness in its suchness to incarnate from, as *avatara*. If he forgets who he is? (Very quantum; the nonlocal memory is indeed potentiality. It has to be triggered in order to crystallise.) Therefore, they decide to send *Radha* along a little before *Krishna* - *Radha* is the archetype of Love. They incarnate, and *Radha*, who is seven years older in their incarnate bodies, helps *Krishna* to remember who he is, guides *Krishna* through his adolescence until he is ready to establish *Dharma* in the rest of the World.

This is too prosaic and does not satisfy the romantic. Another myth was then created, in which *Krishna* and *Radha* are romantic lovers. Of course, whereas *Radha* loves within a committed relationship, *Krishna's* love is all-inclusive. In this legend, *Krishna* had *Radha* as a lover, but he also had ten thousand of other lovers. And of course, *Radha* is often depicted as jealous in some legends. Much misunderstood; *Radha's* love is quite unconditional.

How can *Krishna* satisfy all those women? Still another legend explains. This is about the legendary love of *Krishna* and his *gopis* (Sanskrit word for consorts) celebrated in the *Hindu Vaishnavite* tradition. On special full moon nights, *Krishna* dances with his ten thousand *gopis*, all at once. Or so the legend goes. Can *Krishna* duplicate himself in ten thousand bodies? If you think of *Krishna's* love as love in space and time as in a brain circuit, you will be puzzled by this legend. It must be a metaphor! It is. The unconditional as well as inclusive love of *Krishna* is always celebrated outside of space and time, nonlocally, as relationships with the potentiality of tangled hierarchy that can be manifest with anyone that comes in your sphere of living.

Tying It All Up

This is not the first time an attempt has been made to define a spiritual path for worldly people. Bhagavad Gita, that delivers what Krishna, the *avatara*, had to say to the worldly human Arjuna in the form of a long song, may be one such attempt.

What you have to notice is that Gita's metaphysics is not the metaphysics of Vedanta, perfect non-dualism, but *Samkhya*, a seemingly dualistic philosophy. If you look with the quantum lens, you easily can see that the Samkhya is really about qualified non-dualism.

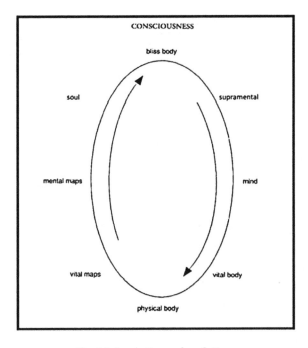

Fig. 16. Involution and evolution

In the quantum worldview, consciousness is the ground of being with scientific subject potentiality and object potentiality in it - *purusha* and *prakriti* respectively in the language of Samkhya. The metaphysics of the Bhagavad Gita is the same as the quantum worldview. And Gita indeed tries to integrate epistemology as well: all the disparate paths to spirituality that people were using at the time - variously called raja yoga, karma yoga, bhakti yoga, and gyana yoga.

The next attempt at an integration was made by Sri Aurobindo. Aurobindo not only tried to integrate an integrative epistemology that he called Integral yoga but also a complete new metaphysics balancing the transcendent and the immanent. Philosophically speaking, the Vedantic nondualism is correct; the ultimate reality is eternal; it never changes; here nothing can happen. For something to happen, Aurobindo sees the necessity of involution - creation of limitation. The first limitation is consciousness with qualifications - sat, chit, ananda. Then come the potentialities of consciousness - the subtle. Then finally matter in potentiality with complete inertness at the macro level as far as consciousness is concerned; but macro matter can make representation of consciousness and its various aspects and attributes such as the subtle. Evolution then is seen as an evolution of representation-making (fig. 16) involving creativity and quantum leaps as explained in Amit's book *Creative Evolution*. All fits.

It is said that Sri Aurobindo had an experience of inclusive Love when he was in a British jail in Kolkata, waiting for a verdict on a charge of terrorism against him. Aurobindo saw everyone as *Vasudeva* - another name of *Krishna* - as Wholeness, inclusive Love. He developed his insightful integrative philosophy on the basis of this experience and the power of intuition and creative insights.

We are no Aurobindo, certainly no Krishna, but to fill in our deficiencies we had the help of quantum physics, wisdom traditions, results of hard practice and experimental data. Third time should be the charm.

BIBLIOGRAPHY

- Aurobindo, Sri. *The Synthesis of Yoga.* Pondichery, India: Aurobindo Ashram.

- Aurobindo, Sri. (1996). *The Life Divine.* Pondicherry, India: Sri Aurobindo Ashram.

- Goswami, A. (1993). *The Self-Aware Universe: How Consciousness Creates the Material World.* N.Y.:Tarcher/ Putnam.

- Goswami, A. (2000). *The Visionary Window: A Quantum Physicist's Guide to Enlightenment.* Wheaton, IL: Quest Books.

- Goswami, A. (2001). *Physics of the Soul.* Charlottsville, VA: Hampton Roads.

- Goswami, A. (2004). *The Quantum Doctor.* Charlottsville, VA: Hampton Roads.

- Goswami, A. (2008). *God is not Dead.* Charlottsville, VA: Hampton Roads.

- Goswami, A. (2008). *Creative Evolution.* Wheaton, IL: Theosophical Publishing House.

- Goswami, A. (2011). *How Quantum Activism can save Civilization.* Charlotts ville, VA: Hampton Roads

- Goswami, A. (2014). *Quantum Creativity: Think Quantum, Be Creative.* N. Y.: Hay House.

- Goswami, A. (2017). *The Everything Answer Book.* Charlottesville, VA: Hampton Roads.

- Pert, C. (1997). *Molecules of Emotion.* N.Y.: Scribner.

- Radin, D. (2009). *The Noetic Universe*. London: Transworld Publishers.
- Searle, J. (1994). *The Rediscovery of the Mind*. Cambridge, MA: MIT Press.
- Teilhard de Chardin, P. (1961). *The Phenomenon of Man*. N.Y.: Harper & Row.
- Wilber, K. *The Atman Proje*ct.

INDEX

Amit Goswami, PhD

Amit is a retired professor of physics at the University of Oregon (1968 - 1997).

He discovered the solution to the quantum measurement problem and developed a science of experience explicating how consciousness splits into subject and object in 1985.

Subsequently, he developed a theory of reincarnation and integrated conventional and alternative medicine within the new quantum science of health. Among his discoveries are the quantum theory of the creative process, the theory of quantum evolution, and the theory of quantum economics that extends Adam's Smith's capitalism into a workable paradigm for the 21st century.

In 2009, he started a movement called "quantum activism", now gaining ground in North and South America, Southern and Eastern Europe, and India. In 2018, together with his collaborators, he established Quantum Activism Vishwalayam, an institution of transformative education in India, based on quantum science and the primacy of consciousness.

He is the author of numerous books, most notably: *The Self-Aware Universe, Physics of the Soul, The Quantum Doctor, God is Not Dead, Quantum Creativity, and The Everything Answer Book.* He was featured in the movie *What the Bleep Do We Know*, and the documentaries *Dalai Lama Renaissance,* and *The Quantum Activist.*

Amit is a spiritual practitioner and calls himself a quantum activist in search of Wholeness.

Valentina R. Onisor, MD

Valentina is a practicing physician specialized in family medicine, who integrates various systems of alternative medicine (acupuncture, Ayurveda, naturopathy, tachyon) into her practice. Involved in consciousness awakening related sciences for two decades, a pioneer of quantum integrative medicine, she is also a yoga and meditation teacher (Mahasiddha Yoga, Sivananda Vedanta Forest Academy, Yoga Alliance, Universal Consciousness Ambassador CSETI). She has made correlations between the ancient genuine sciences and quantum physics, using them as support for her workshops, classes and lectures that are oriented towards healing and spiritual transformation.

Over years, Valentina has developed great empathy towards human suffering and understanding of the subtle causes of disease. Through a unique system of Quantum Healing, she inspires people to achieve enhanced physical, emotional and spiritual health that allows for profound and long-lasting transformation and regeneration on all levels.

As a co-leader in transformational education, Dr. Onisor serves as the Dean of Students at Quantum Activism Vishwalayam, an international institution of higher transformative education headquartered in India. She is a lecturer at Quantum Academy in Brazil. She has been an acting consultant for the CQA in Oregon, USA since 2016. Valentina is co-author (along with Amit Goswami, PhD) of the upcoming books: *How You Can be Your Own Quantum Doctor,* and *The Quantum Science of Love.*

CPSIA information can be obtained
at www.ICGtesting.com
Printed in the USA
LVHW081021041219
639394LV00015B/615/P

9 789353 479336